Second Edition

Going Bohemian

How to Teach Writing Like You Mean It

Lawrence Baines &
Anthony Kunkel

**INTERNATIONAL
READING ASSOCIATION**

TM

800 BARKSDALE ROAD, PO BOX 8139
NEWARK, DE 19714-8139, USA
www.reading.org

The International Reading Association attempts, through its publications, to provide a forum for a wide spectrum of opinions on reading. This policy permits divergent viewpoints without implying the endorsement of the Association.

Executive Editor, Books   Corinne M. Mooney
Developmental Editor   Charlene M. Nichols
Developmental Editor   Tori Mello Bachman
Developmental Editor   Stacey L. Reid
Editorial Production Manager   Shannon T. Fortner
Design and Composition Manager   Anette Schuetz

Project Editors   Tori Mello Bachman and Susanne Viscarra

Cover   Design, Lise Holliker Dykes; Images, © Shutterstock

The publisher would appreciate notification where errors occur so that they may be corrected in subsequent printings and/or editions.

Library of Congress Cataloging-in-Publication Data
Going bohemian: how to teach writing like you mean it / Lawrence Baines & Anthony J. Kunkel. — 2nd ed.
     p. cm.
   Includes bibliographical references.
   ISBN 978-0-87207-830-7 (alk. paper)
   1. Creative writing (Secondary education)—United States. 2. English language—Composition and exercises—Study and teaching (Secondary)—United States. I. Baines, Lawrence. II. Kunkel, Anthony.
   LB1631.G615 2010
   808'.0420712—dc22

                                                                                          2010013955

Contents

SECTION 1   15

Basic Footwork: Learning Technique

About the Authors

 **Lawrence Baines** is a professor of English education at The University of Oklahoma in Norman, Oklahoma, USA. He was formerly the holder of the Judith Daso Herb Endowed Chair at The University of Toledo in Toledo, Ohio, USA, and the G. Leland Green Endowed Chair in Education at Berry College in Rome, Georgia, USA. He began his teaching career as a wonk, but after 20 years of working with apathetic, oppositional, and absolutely brilliant adolescents, he decided to go bohemian. For more information, see www.lawrencebaines.com. You can contact him at lbaines@ou.edu.

 **Anthony Kunkel** currently teaches high school English in the San Francisco Bay area. He began his teaching career in the mid-1990s in rural Florida, where he began focusing on building a curriculum that challenged a standardized approach to teaching kids to write. He has since taught English at several high schools and colleges from Florida to California, worked as a curriculum consultant for Florida and Georgia, and has taught the curriculum credential courses for the California State University system. You can contact him at anthonykunkel@sfhs.com.

Introduction

Anything is a structure. If we presuppose that some things are structures and other things are substantive elements which go into structures, we have trapped ourselves at the outset. Everything is both, which is to say that things and relations are matters of conceptual option. To understand the option one is playing one must be aware of where one has mentally placed himself.

From *Teaching the Universe of Discourse* by James Moffet

"Exactly what is your theoretical framework? As a teacher, you must be well grounded in a theoretical framework, or you simply will not be able to function effectively in the classroom."

The words of the professor in your graduate class ring in your ears as you drive home in the dark. You think to yourself, theoretical framework? Just this afternoon, Angel Gutierrez (all names are pseudonyms) screamed, "Go to hell, bitch!" in fifth period when you asked him to take his seat. Then, Wes Abbott, the autistic kid who has been up and down on different medications all year, started walking around the room, trying to turn over everyone's desk, while two girls started shoving each other at the back of the room. In the midst of the chaos, the counselor knocked on your door to introduce a new student to the class—Yue Bang, from China. Yue seemed bright, but she did not speak English and was living temporarily with her brother and sister at a nearby church. You might appreciate discussing the nuances of theoretical frameworks if you didn't have one or two things already occupying your gray matter.

Perhaps it was insane to sign up for a graduate class at night while you held down a full-time teaching position. Perhaps you should have simply gone for the quick and easy Internet degree like everyone else. (What did your colleague say about her Internet courses the other day? She googled two articles, signed on to a chat room for 15 minutes, and received an A.) But, you wanted to become a better teacher, so you signed up at the university in the hope that you might learn something of value. Was it a mistake?

You just finished the first week of school, and it had been the usual pandemonium of textbook distribution, seating charts, overcrowded classrooms, and interminable faculty meetings. Your fingers are ink-stained in red, your hair is beyond hope, and the odor of sweaty, hormone-crazed adolescents seems to waft in the air everywhere you go.

As you think about your school day, it seems that you barely had enough time for a bathroom break, let alone time to reflect on the extent to which you are a facilitative, student-centered, empowering teacher. Besides having to read six sets of compositions over the weekend, you are looking into buying a home, you must work on getting a billing problem settled with your cell phone company, and you have to buy your mother a gift for her birthday, which was actually last week. There was also something else you wanted to address that had to do with your social life. Let's see, what was it? Oh yes, you wanted to have one.

One thing is certain: This weekend you won't have time to sit around, pontificate, and go through the academic exercise of lining up an abstruse, fictitious theoretical framework. You decide that you will slap down something scholarly sounding at the last minute to pacify the professor. For now, you are focused on what to do in class tomorrow morning.

Remember when you first decided to become a teacher? You wanted to change lives, to teach so that it mattered—to your students, to the community, to the world.

Okay, you admit it. You want Angel Gutierrez to care. You want Wes Abbott to become so absorbed in the day's activities that he might forget about turning over desks. You want Yue Bang to get a sense of the wonder, joy, and immense power of learning. You want everyone in your classes to learn to love literature, to become avid readers for the rest of their lives, to become accomplished writers and thinkers, to show tolerance for each other, and to work with indefatigable enthusiasm every day.

You have no time to waste, so you've decided to go bohemian.

On Assessment

It was early on in my first year of teaching that I realized how little I knew about the assessment of student writing. After a rough beginning, I finally began to transform my class into a writing environment. As the students became more receptive to writing, their papers began increasing in length and, particularly, in tone.

There was a quiet 14-year-old girl in one of my morning classes who never smiled, even though she always did everything I asked and did it very well. My class had been writing rough drafts for reflective essays, and I had requested that they reflect on a memory that carried some powerful emotions. On the second day of writing, I noticed the tears falling onto this young girl's paper. When I moved closer to her, she leaned over her paper, but continued to write. I knelt beside her and asked her quietly if she would consider writing about something less painful. She shook her head faintly, almost imperceptibly, and continued writing.

On the third day of writing the reflective essays, the students were put into groups for peer critiques. As I handed out my guidelines, the girl informed me that she did not want to let anyone read her essay. I felt that it might do her some good to get the feedback, so I told her not to be shy and that she should get used to letting others critique her work. For a moment she sat there shaking her head, then she abruptly grabbed her paper and walked out of class. Stunned, I quickly followed after her. She was standing there crying, and without a word, she handed me her crumpled essay. I began reading her story. It was beautiful.

She described the ride from her mom's house to her uncle's with all the wonder and excitement of an 8-year-old child. The imagery was vivid: She wrote that the sun woke up the flowers that lined her uncle's driveway, and she described the fragrance of jasmine through the senses of a child. She was saddened to bid farewell to her mother. I was shocked to read the description of her torment and confusion as her uncle viciously raped her for the first time. Although her story was terrifying, her writing was lovely. She used long compound sentences for description, followed by short powerful sentences for effect. As I walked her to the guidance counselor's office, I wondered how I would put a grade on a paper like this. I never did, but in my grade book I put an A.

When students write, they are only equal in that they are individuals. Writing is individual. Assessment of writing, therefore, needs to be individual as well. Just as the student who has to struggle for every word in every sentence deserves one grade, the gifted writer who makes no effort to write beyond the simplest expectations deserves another. If assessing writing were a sure thing, there would be a great deal more writing in English classrooms. The reality of a typical classroom today is diversity, and given the nature of this diversity, the writing teacher has to create a rubric of expectations. It is unlikely that a standard, five-paragraph essay will require the same criteria as a prose passage that calls for images to be used as central metaphors. It is up to the teacher to decide exactly what is expected with each piece.

Assessment has been researched extensively, and perhaps the most comprehensive information available will point a person toward holistic evaluation. However, the teacher who chooses to really make his or her students write ultimately must find a comfort zone that allows for teacher feedback as well as assessment.

For the teacher who encourages his or her 120 to 180 students to write 15 to 20 pages a week, it could be assumed that there will be an abundance of assessment needed, but this is not necessarily so. Does it make sense to have students write less so that all work may be graded or commented on? If they are writing more and I am still providing as much, if not more, feedback than if they were writing less, does it matter if I have not read every word they have written?

I believe it is the writing that counts, not the amount of reading I do. I have heard other English teachers state that they read every word their students write. I could spend countless hours attempting to read everything I have my students write, but that would become frustrating, and I would more than likely ask them to write less. I have a standard policy in my classes: *Everything that is written is subject to a grade, but not everything written will receive one.* I use an abundance of skill-building activities in class, and during these I work with the students, answering questions and providing feedback as they write. Usually I follow such activities with a major assignment that puts the new skills into practice. These assignments usually have no length requirements, but I ask the students to limit their writing to under 20 pages, unless they feel that is impossible. At the beginning of the year, there is always apprehension, but it doesn't take long for even the most reluctant of writers to realize that some pieces require extensive development.

On longer assignments, I generally have a rubric in mind or written out of my expectations, and I provide the students with these expectations at the onset of the assignment. While grading, I make a point to mark only on the first three pages and then focus in as a holistic reader. Because most assignments are completed during class, I am familiar with specific problems each writer has had and questions they have asked. Individuality and effort always count.

For many assignments, I incorporate oral presentations into the grading. Oral presentations are a useful vehicle for students to share work with peers, and they allow the teacher to provide instant feedback. I have found that by not forcing the students to read their work aloud, more often than not they are more receptive to doing so.

To address the worry of some students that I may have overlooked some of their better work, I also incorporate a portfolio into my grading. Each grading term, which is nine weeks in my school, I require the students to put together selected pieces that they are particularly proud of, especially work that was done in class but not recognized. This works well in two ways: First, it lets students know that their best work can be counted as a grade, even if it was not one of the graded assignments, and second, it allows me an opportunity to pick and choose what I wish to grade without worrying that I will have missed a significant piece of writing by any of my students.

However you choose to assess students' work, it is important to reconsider the stigmatic tradition of grading everything that is ever written in class. Students today, more than ever, need to write. Moving past the simplicity of "process writing" and teaching students to write instinctively will enhance both the quality of their writing and the quality of their discovery. Once a student experiences hearing his or her own writer's voice, he or she will find it frustrating to accept anything less than quality. Writing at this point becomes very personal.

Several years ago, I was teaching writing classes at a high school in rural northern Florida. Like many schools in the state, it had become hostage to the "grading" system that the state had implemented. This school scored a D the previous year, which was the catalyst for the writing courses. It was my first year there, and the school had asked that I create and implement a class that would improve the scores for the "Florida Writes" portion of the testing. As it was, all ninth graders would take a semester course on writing through me or the one other teacher who would help teach the course. I was excited. It was where I started as a teacher. When school began and I was able to shut my door and teach, it was fantastic. Professionally, though, it was an ill environment. There was pressure on the school to produce results, or the school would be taken over by appointed authorities.

These students also took their regular English class, so my focus was to be voice and development. In this, I was very successful. The following year when my students were tested, they scored well above the average for the state. Within two years, ninth graders at the school were among the highest scoring students in the state in writing.

Over the years, I have worked the full spectrum in education: high school teacher, dean, curriculum principal, college lecturer, and credential curriculum teacher. Sadly enough, through many school and teacher observations, I have come to understand why there is a need for some teachers to be given a standardized curriculum. It is intended to create an equal experience for the students, and probably for the teachers as well. It's supposed to make assessments easier and problems easier to identify. However, although such a proposition sounds logical, it is impossible as long as humans continue to do the teaching. Just as students learn differently, teachers teach differently. Students are highly idiosyncratic and need to be addressed as individuals. Equally important, a teacher must consider his or her own strengths with regard to writing and reading.

What I have found to be consistently useful in grading and assessment is to have the assessment I plan to use figured out well before I begin teaching whatever it is I'm teaching. Teaching is the journey, but your assessment is the destination. The final assessment is when the students are able to show you what they understand with regard to what you have taught them.

In the past, this idea has been called performance assessment or authentic assessment, but the problem with any kind of assessment is that it sometimes gets in the way of learning. Writing does not always need formal assessment. Some students will learn to write simply because they find it good therapy.

Often the activities and projects I do in my classes, many of which are in this book, are the assessments I use to determine how well the students understand what I've been teaching. I've heard the talk among the students: "Mr. K. doesn't give tests," but that's not entirely true. I don't give the students multiple-choice or true–false tests. I don't give study guides or 100-question exams. Instead, I offer students options and choices on how they will show me what they have learned. I want students to think creatively about how to express and apply what they have learned.

Anthony Kunkel

From a Student

A former teacher of mine recently asked me to write about what I experience on a typical day in the classroom. I thought about this for some time and decided that I'd like to give you a tangible sense of how students see the classroom and the teachers running those classes. This is a view from the flip side. The faces peering from behind the desk are more than just scenery.

Fourth Period

I walk into class, my mind buzzing with the social static I picked up in the halls. I hail some friends and slide into my seat, ready to make my grade for the day. The teacher rises languidly from his desk and stands to face the class. He gazes at us tiredly for a moment, then moves to the board to write our assignment for the day: page 290 (1–7), 297 (1–12). Book work again—oh boy. The teacher returns to his seat and begins scratching at some papers with a stubby red pencil. Some of the students open their books, but most begin in friendly conversation. Quickly the conversation turns to loud talking, then progresses to some yells and laughing. The teacher slams his pencil down and jumps from his desk like a jack-in-the-box. "Be quiet and do the assignment or I'm gonna start writing people up!" he shouts while waving a pink slip at us, the same one he's waved all year. The class becomes quiet, paying lip service to his authority, and a few more students open their books.

I look up one answer after another. Henry V, Battle of Hastings, Industrial Revolution—these are just names, words. That's all the book asks for. I copy a passage, rewrite a sentence, and look for a keyword or phrase, one after another. I find it in the book and write it on paper. The only thing I know about the Battle of Hastings is that it's the answer to number 5. Occasionally I don't answer a question completely. No big deal; I doubt he'll read it anyway.

When I finish, I walk up to the teacher's desk and lay the paper on the small stack that has already been finished. His head never lifts, and his pencil continues to slash red across words and numbers. Some in the class read faster than I do and are already finished. They have moved to the back of the class and pulled out the cards—rummy today, or spades. I glance at the clock; we have 20 minutes left. Most students haven't finished yet, and some haven't even begun. They are waiting for a friend to finish so they can copy their answers. They aren't really cheating, just increasing the efficiency of their writing. They'll learn the same whether they copy from a book or from a friend. I lay my head down and sleep. Soon the bell rings, and I leave class knowing nothing more about Henry V than I did when I walked in—except that he's the answer to number 3.

Fifth Period

I take my seat, journal ready, and wait for the bell. A few stragglers slide in just before the bell and grab their journals from the box, then move straight to their seats. The teacher stands at his podium in front of the class, watching as the desks fill. When the bell rings we speak quietly as he takes roll. One brave soul slips over to a neighboring table and the teacher pauses and asks, "Michael, what are you doing?" Michael shakes his head, embarrassed, and skitters back to his desk. The teacher finishes taking roll then greets the class. Most have their journals open with a pen or pencil ready. "Alright, everyone, you know the deal. Let's spend about 10 minutes on the journals, then we'll move on."

The class quietly bends to the task. This is always one of my favorite parts. We write, sometimes on a topic, sometimes not. There is no sound but pencils moving. The room is like a cathedral. No one talks and no one stops writing. To speak during journals would be akin to heresy. When the teacher finally breaks the silence with a single "OK," there is a palpable sigh, and subdued voices start up again, still low, but now permissible. It doesn't take long, however, for the students' attention to become focused on the man standing in front of the class. My neighbor and I exchange a few words, but are quickly caught in a wave of "shush" that comes from our classmates.

The teacher has us wrapped around his finger, and he knows it. He stares at the class for a moment, looking from face to face, then smiles. "Today we are going to begin writing screenplays," he says.

Yesterday it was commercials. Last week, we studied and created metaphors. Every day it's something new. The class waits, anticipating, wondering how, knowing he'll tell us. Everyone gets involved; you cannot slip by in this class, and we all know it. Even those who come to school just to get out of the house participate.

I watch him in front of the class, describing narrative styles as if he's preaching the Gospel, and look around at the class. Everyone is watching the overhead projector, watching his writing flow across the screen, making it look simple. It never is, though. He makes sure of it. This class is for thinking. He's not a stickler for spelling or grammar; it's all about creation.

Today's screenplays are just one plank of a bridge that he's teaching us to build. As he nears the end of his instructions, the class becomes jittery. We know that shortly he'll set us free to run with the ideas he's inspired. It's like he's turned on the tap and our ideas have begun to flow. Each of us begins to create. The class begins discussing ideas for their screenplays. Our small groups within the class have become competitive with the other groups, and we all wish to outdo each other. The teacher wanders from group to group, jumping into conversations and bouncing ideas off of us, sometimes so hard it hurts. The hush in the class disappears, replaced by the buzz of creation.

No one I know can inspire this amount of zeal into my normally sluggish classmates. He has plowed our minds through careful practice of each skill, each technique, and each mindset necessary to write the way he expects us to. And we *want* to write as well as he expects us to. We've learned point-of-view writing, mood writing, description, and persuasion. We've practiced writing everything from short stories to radio jingles, from poems to magazine ads, but at this moment knowledge steps aside and ability begins to take over; he is teaching us instincts. We can feel a good sentence, use metaphors without noticing, and know immediately when a piece of writing needs a revision. The difference between good and bad writing, independent from any rules or guidelines, has become clear.

I pause in mid-paragraph to consider a phrase, rework it in my mind, knowing I can make it better, and the bell rings. I look at the clock for the first time since class has started. It seems as if we have just begun. As I put my work away and begin preparing for my next class, I'm still reworking the phrase in my mind.

Rob Jones
11th grade
Dixie County High School
Cross City, Florida, USA
1998

From a Student, 12 Years On

I Write for a Living. My Writing Tastes Like Dust.

Years ago, before laptops became our notepads and when literature was an adventure and a chore, I wrote the intro to the first edition of this book with a Bic Round-Stick Medium black pen, on college-ruled paper. And it tasted magnificent.

But I suppose some context is in order.

The book you're holding is the result of years of experimentation, innovation, failures, and introspection, all conducted by two guys who stood in front of classrooms and tried to pull words from the minds of adolescents. I was one of those kids, with a callus on the middle finger of my right hand permanently smudged with ink (gone now—laptops, remember?), who through mayhem and trickery ended up authoring an intro about what it was like to be a high school student in a writing class. I called it "a view from the flip side." I wrote about being captivated by a lesson plan, by an atmosphere, and ultimately by a teacher who broke the rules and asked each and every one of his students to give all that they had. Some didn't. But, many of us did. And now, years later, I no longer remember high school with such clarity, yet I find myself rubbing that spot on the middle finger of my right hand, where the impression of the pen once sat. There are things I remember.

I put together words every day, strung into sentences splashed across screens, sent electronically to coworkers and students and the vast word pile that is the Unending Internet. I am a social scientist, of sorts, and work in an academic setting that lends itself to dry, structured writing that is there to *do a job*. Usually to explain. Occasionally to persuade. And once in a while, a paragraph or two to excite. Now, don't get me wrong—I love what I do—but rereading the thoughts of my high school self reminds me of the power of words. Not just to crumble empires and change the world. Not to pull a tear from an eye or light an audience on fire. I am reminded of the power that writing has to teach us about ourselves.

What I wrote about years ago, as a high school junior and future Hemingway (of course), was not really about writing well. Sure, product is important. In this book, you'll read a bit about assessing the written word, the task of grading, about which much ink has been spilled. But teaching writing isn't about producing students who can produce a product. If it were, then we'd all be content to drill the five-paragraph essay until our students could reproduce it like perfect little automatons. What I wrote about a decade ago, and what I remember about fifth-period high school composition, is *atmosphere, process,* and *instinct.*

What sets a good writing class apart from the hours of drab high school desk time is the atmosphere the teacher creates—a space where writing is both creative and challenging, where even a skilled student can't look ahead and see the right answer. Sitting down with a blank sheet of paper felt for me like facing the *unknown.* My writing class was unpredictable, unorthodox, *bohemian.* We never knew what was coming—screenplays, radio jingles, peer reviews (still terrifying after all these years)—the class was many things, but never mundane. For a high schooler, whose every hour is governed by bells, a little unpredictability went a long way.

Rarely in high school are students asked to spend much time with any one thing. There is a linearity to course work—moving through chapters, through time periods, through techniques—that lends itself to shallowness. But a good course on writing can't be satisfied with moving from skill to skill, because writing is a *process.* Being asked to go back to something you'd written, to mull it over, to improve it, was a novelty. We never revised our math tests.

But being forced to rework drafts, ours and others, taught patience and engagement with the maddening process of crafting the correct words. In a place where too much time is spent on finding the one right answer, being asked to rewrite, revise, and *rethink* meant engaging with the subject at a deeper level. It was a shock the first time I turned in an *obviously* perfect story, just to be told to do it again, do it differently, *do it better.* The emphasis was not on the words but the process of discovering them, and it is a process that I've since spent years engaged with. Not every high schooler will write for a living. But learning the lesson of *doing something well* is valuable for everyone, and it is something that I remember.

I never did get good at typing. My fingers don't fly to the keys the way they should, and at this point, I've accepted that. If I had worked at it more, I'm sure they'd find the keyboard without so much glancing down. Typing reminds me of the cramps in my hand that I'd shake out after bending tightly over a notepad, my Bic scraping furiously for an hour. We wrote *a lot*. I write a lot now, but it is at my own pace, on a keyboard, and doesn't cause the cramps or the ink stains that it did back then. Any craftsman knows the role of muscle memory, of *instinct,* in doing one's job well. They say that instinct can't be taught, but I think that's crap. Instinct is learned by doing, over and over, but never in quite the same way. We didn't fill pages with words just to make our hands sore, but now sore hands are *familiar territory.* Today, I know when a sentence comes out clunky, even if I don't know why. I ended high school having written scary stories, ads, obituaries, novels. Which means I have no fear of curriculum vitae, e-mails, term papers, love poems. By casting the net wide, by stretching the boundaries, my high school writing class taught us *instincts* rather than skills. Skills can get dull or be forgotten with time. Instincts are forever.

Contrary to what you may have heard, not all teachers *can* be bohemians. Just as not every one of your students will become professional writers. My views on the importance of writing might be biased by my choice of career paths (or did they bias my path?), but I'll be honest—high school is a blur for me. I recall a vague sense of anxiousness, boredom, and the feeling that the hoops I was jumping through were for someone else's enjoyment. But freshman composition was a different story. It was challenging, frustrating, infuriating, and exhilarating in a way that algebra and history were not. It was a different space, conducted by a different kind of person, than the other hour-long periods that made up my day. The teacher was difficult, hard to satisfy, easily excited, and impossible to predict. His lesson plans were unorthodox, exhausting, torturous, and fun.

Those lesson plans, and ones like them, are in this book for you to explore. Tweak 'em. Change 'em. Use 'em as springboards for something new. Challenge your students to go beyond expectations and they will soar. My high school writing teacher was a *bohemian,* and his lessons have endured. Will yours?

Rob Jones
PhD student in archaeology
University of Arizona
2010

Basic Footwork: Learning Technique

*When you're practicing deeply, the world's usual rules are
suspended. You use time more efficiently. Your small efforts
produce big, lasting results. You have positioned yourself at
a place of leverage where you can capture failure and turn
it into skill. The trick is to choose a goal just beyond your
present abilities; to target the struggle.*

From *The Talent Code: Greatness Isn't Born.
It's Grown. Here's How.* by Daniel Coyle

Every year it's the same. During the first week of school, after a
honeymoon period of maybe 15 minutes, teachers begin lamenting
that students have lost the abilities to write and think.

"What do they teach them in ___ [fill in the blank with the current
grade level of the students minus one] grade?"

"I have never had students like these! These kids can't even write a
complete sentence."

It's easy to blame shoddy writing on previous teachers, students'
intellectual shortcomings, family upbringing, or the weather. However,
the fact remains that adolescents are still developing—as writers and as
human beings. If students were all masterful auteurs when they walked in
the door on the first day of class, they wouldn't need you.

You read *The Talent Code* (Coyle, 2009) and *Talent Is Overrated* (Colvin,
2008), and you understand the importance of practice and modeling in the
development of proficiency. Apparently, Mozart's earliest compositions
were merely copycat pieces, containing musical patterns borrowed
from other composers (Gladwell, 2008). Imitation is not evil, but a logical

starting point. Coldplay learned from The Beatles; The Beatles learned from Elvis; Elvis learned from Hank Snow.

Everyone has to begin somewhere.

You cannot expect students to write well unless you explicitly teach them how. They will not progress as writers if you ask them to fill in blanks or complete multiple-choice exams. Students learn how to write by writing—and writing often.

So, you decide to make like Mozart and encourage your students to learn composing techniques from the masters. Rather than place a literary work on a pedestal, you have your students knock it around the block instead. Eventually, they try out the techniques for themselves. At the least, they will begin to consider technique from the perspective of both reader and writer.

One of the problems with schools today is that everyone—both teachers and students—seems continually frazzled and ultraserious. However, as anyone who has lived through Psych 101 knows, stress obstructs creativity. Fear inhibits learning.

To get students going, you need to loosen them up. So, you assure them that they are in a safe, structured environment, and then you engage them in hours of practice, practice, and more practice. To get students to participate voluntarily, of course, requires that the activity be enjoyable or interesting.

Fortunately, *enjoyable* and *interesting* happen to be your specialties.

RESOURCES

Colvin, G. (2008). *Talent is overrated: What really separates world-class performers from everybody else.* New York: Portfolio.

Coyle, D. (2009). *The talent code: Greatness isn't born. It's grown. Here's how.* New York: Bantam Dell.

Gladwell, M. (2008). *Outliers: The story of success.* New York: Little, Brown.

Performance Art Poetry

Type of Activity
Individual

Approximate Time
One 50-minute class period

Objective
Students will use writing prompts to create a dense, eloquent poem about their hometowns.

Summary
Performance Art Poetry provides some structure for students who otherwise might not participate fully in writing poetry or selecting vibrant, descriptive words.

Materials
Pen and paper, and copies of the Hometown Instructions handout (see p. 20)

If you choose to pursue the Enrichment activity, which is highly recommended, then other supplies, such as a computer, may come into play. However, the exercise may be completed using only pen and paper.

Setup
Begin class by asking students informally about where they grew up. You might want to ask for a show of hands on how many students were born and grew up in the city or town in which they are living now. Allow students to reminisce and tell stories. The idea is to get words flowing. Discuss good aspects and drawbacks about where they are from.

Figure 1. A Student's Performance Art Poetry

Dallas burns
Skyscraper like missile turns
Meat with salsa on the side
Jackhammer overwhelms echoes, "hail the mighty state" inside
Homeless guy holds cardboard sign, pretend cowboy and frantic tycoon
Single mom eight months pregnant lost, stranded 'neath the crazy August moon
Suddenly here now suddenly gone, graceless kiss somehow slithered away too soon
Room without windows, paralyzed face down on the floor
White hair, wrinkled trembling hands, smile behind the door
Never give up, never give up
Sunburn, sweat, and tough
Goes without saying, Dallas plays it rough

Procedure

Tell students that they are going to write a poem about their hometowns. This particular exercise involves you offering a verbal prompt and students responding in writing. Before beginning the activity, however, emphasize that poetry should be expressive, descriptive, and streamlined. Encourage the use of precise, descriptive words and discourage the use of nondescriptive words, such as *big, the, this, it, there.*

Then, distribute and go through the Hometown Instructions handout, one line at a time, and allow students sufficient time to think about a response and write.

After students have completed their initial drafts, have them go back over their poems to identify and replace nondescriptive words. During the editing stage, students may also decide to rework their lines so that they rhyme (as in the student sample in Figure 1), but rhyming is not necessary.

Enrichment

To do any enrichment activities, you should wait until *after* the writing has been completed. Once the poem has been written, you may want to have students link the words in the poem with photographs, music, drawings, or other sensory stimuli. Students can compile everything into a slide show (using PowerPoint or the free version available through www .openoffice.com) or film. If a slide show, I suggest a maximum of one line written out with accompanying image/music per slide. If a film, I suggest having students write out the lines to the poem during the editing process so that the lines of the poem become titles, or having students write out the lines to the poem on an object, then film them. For example, one shot might show a student writing the lines on a blackboard or in a text message.

HOMETOWN INSTRUCTIONS

Write your poem following these guidelines:

Line 1: The place where you grew up and a verb (2 words)

Line 2: The landscape with analogy (4 words)

Line 3: The smell or taste of your hometown (6 words)

Line 4: Music, song, or sounds that remind you of your hometown (8 words)

Line 5: The kind of people who live there (10 words)

Line 6: An important event in your life (12 words)

Line 7: An important event in your life (12 words; You may repeat the above line or write a new one.)

Line 8: A dream or nightmare (10 words)

Line 9: Physical traits of an influential person (8 words)

Line 10: The specific advice or truth someone once gave you (6 words; Perhaps you heard it from the person mentioned above. Try to write out their advice specifically, then delete the quotations marks.)

Line 11: Effects of the weather (4 words)

Line 12: An analogy for your hometown plus a verb and whatever else you feel like throwing in for a last line (2–10 words)

From *Going Bohemian: How to Teach Writing Like You Mean It* (2nd edition) by Lawrence Baines & Anthony Kunkel. Copyright 2010 International Reading Association.

Modeling Prose With Ernie and Jane

Type of Activity
Individual

Approximate Time
One 50-minute class period

Objective
Students will learn how to write in two distinctly different styles: those of authors Ernest Hemingway and Jane Austen. Modeling Prose With Ernie and Jane also shows students how to make their writing more interesting. You may wish to substitute more contemporary writers, such as J.K. Rowling, Thomas Pynchon, Kurt Vonnegut, or Zadie Smith.

Summary
Modeling Prose With Ernie and Jane is especially useful for remedial students and students whose primary language is not English, because it provides a ready-made framework for language. That is, students are able to focus on word selection and the meaning of words rather than building a structure to hold the words from scratch. This activity is a great exercise from which to jump to style, tone, or compare-and-contrast essays.

By adapting the writing style of a different author, students learn to appreciate the highly individualistic nature of writing. After participating in Modeling Prose With Ernie and Jane once or twice, aspects of other writers' styles begin to show up in students' writing. This positive development is usually invisible to all but the teacher who assigned this activity.

Materials
You'll need to be able to read aloud from the literature you select and have copies of prose excerpts to hand out to students before beginning the assignment. You'll also need copies of the Distinctive Style handouts (see

pp. 23 and 24), which include excerpts from the works of Hemingway and Austen.

Setup

Tell students that they are going to learn different ways to express themselves using two distinctive styles.

Procedure

Give students a copy of the Distinctive Style: Ernie handout. Have students read the Hemingway excerpt silently, then ask one to read it aloud. Ask students to note sentence length, use of adjectives, frequency of clauses, and repetition.

Ask the class to help write a few sample sentences in Hemingway's style on the board or a transparency. Note the stylistic choices of the sentences and make sure that students truly understand Hemingway's style: minimal use of adjectives, frequent use of repetition, subject–verb sentence structure, relatively short sentence length.

If students get it, then they try writing Hemingway's style on their own. Students read their compositions aloud. Teacher writes the best student sentences on the board or overhead and corrects writing that does not adhere to Hemingway's style. Ask students to note sentence length, use of adjectives, frequency of clauses, dialogue, and repetition in their writing.

Give students a copy of the Distinctive Style: Jane handout. Follow the protocol established with the Hemingway piece.

Enrichment

As readers of the original *Going Bohemian* know, this activity was originally presented using models by John Grisham, Sue Grafton, and Thomas Pynchon. In fact, you should choose models based on specific goals. For instance, if you want students to add more description to their writing, you could use passages from Dickens or Poe; a teacher who wants students to use more precise vocabulary might choose passages from contemporary nonfiction writers Atul Gawande or Steven Pinker.

DISTINCTIVE STYLE: ERNIE

<u>Excerpt from *A Farewell to Arms* by Ernest Hemingway:</u>

Catherine had a good time in the time of pregnancy. It wasn't bad. She was hardly ever sick. She was not awfully uncomfortable until towards the last. So now they got her in the end. You never got away with anything. Get away hell! It would have been the same if we had been married fifty times. And what if she should die. She won't die. People don't die in childbirth nowadays. That was what all husbands thought. Yes, but what if she should die. She won't die. She's just having a bad time.

Excerpted from *A Farewell to Arms*, by E. Hemingway, 1995, New York: Scribner, p. 227.

<u>Assignment:</u>

Rewrite the passage in Hemingway's style, using an incident of your own (real or imagined) involving, for example, life at school, incidents at a party, choosing what to wear, or having dinner.

From *Going Bohemian: How to Teach Writing Like You Mean It* (2nd edition) by Lawrence Baines & Anthony Kunkel. Copyright 2010 International Reading Association.

DISTINCTIVE STYLE: JANE

<u>Excerpt from *Pride and Prejudice* by Jane Austen:</u>

It is a truth universally acknowledged, that a single man in possession of a good fortune, must be in want of a wife.

However little known the feelings or views of such a man may be on his first entering a neighbourhood, this truth is so well fixed in the minds of the surrounding families, that he is considered as the rightful property of some one or other of their daughters.

"My dear Mr. Bennet," said his lady to him one day, "have you heard that Netherfield Park is let at last?"

Mr. Bennet replied that he had not.

"But it is," returned she; "for Mrs. Long has just been here, and she told me all about it."

Mr. Bennet made no answer.

"Do not you want to know who has taken it?" cried his wife impatiently.

"*You* want to tell me, and I have no objection to hearing it."

This was invitation enough.

"Why, my dear, you must know, Mrs. Long says that Netherfield is taken by a young man of large fortune from the north of England; that he came down on Monday in a chaise and four to see the place, and was so much delighted with it that he agreed with Mr. Morris immediately; that he is to take possession before Michaelmas, and some of his servants are to be in the house by the end of next week."

"What is his name?"

"Bingley."

"Is he married or single?"

"Oh! single, my dear, to be sure! A single man of large fortune; four or five thousand a year. What a fine thing for our girls!"

"How so? how can it affect them?"

"My dear Mr. Bennet," replied his wife, "how can you be so tiresome! You must know that I am thinking of his marrying one of them."

"Is that his design in settling here?"

"Design! nonsense, how can you talk so! But it is very likely that he *may* fall in love with one of them, and therefore you must visit him as soon as he comes."

Excerpted from *Pride and Prejudice*, by J. Austen, 2006, New York: Cambridge University Press, pp. 3–4.

<u>Assignment:</u>

Rewrite the passage, keeping Austen's style. Use dialogue, but make the discussion of possible match-making reflective of contemporary life.

The 128-Word Sentence

Type of Activity
Individual or group

Approximate Time
Half of one 50-minute class period

Objective
Students will use clauses and phrases appropriately to create a legitimate, eloquent, very long sentence.

Summary
The 128-Word Sentence is a great exercise to use when your students' writing seems overly reliant on dull subject–verb–noun structures. The 128-Word Sentence also helps alert students to the possibility of sentence rhythm. For example, in "A Rose for Emily," Faulkner writes several lengthy sentences, but he also writes the following as a single paragraph: "The man himself lay in the bed."

Materials
Pen and paper

Setup
Have samples of very long sentences ready.

Procedure
Read a few long sentences by famous authors. One of my favorites is a 128-word sentence from "A Rose for Emily" by William Faulkner (1987):

> They held the funeral on the second day, with the town coming to look at
> Miss Emily beneath a mass of bought flowers, with the crayon face of her

25

father musing profoundly above the bier and the ladies sibilant and macabre; and the very old men—some in their brushed Confederate uniforms—on the porch and the lawn, talking of Miss Emily as if she had been a contemporary of theirs, believing that they had danced with her and courted her perhaps, confusing time with its mathematical progression, as the old do, to whom all the past is not a diminishing road but, instead, a huge meadow which no winter ever quite touches, divided from them now by the narrow bottle-neck of the most recent decade of years. (p. 258)

Discuss Faulkner's technique. Have students underline prepositions, such as *beneath, with, of, above*, and draw a circle around words that end in *–ing*, such as *believing, confusing*. Discuss how Faulkner uses a variety of phrases within a single sentence.

You may also want to use an example from a more contemporary author, such as Philip Roth (2004), who wrote the following 142-word whopper in *The Plot Against America*:

Elizabeth, New Jersey, when my mother was being raised there in a flat over her father's grocery store, was an industrial port a quarter the size of Newark, dominated by the Irish working class and their politicians and the tightly knit parish life that revolved around the town's many churches, and though I never heard her complain of having been pointedly ill-treated in Elizabeth as a girl, it was not until she married and moved to Newark's new Jewish neighborhood that she discovered the confidence that led her to become first a PTA "grade mother," then a PTA vice president in charge of establishing a Kindergarten Mothers' Club, and finally the PTA president, who, after attending a conference in Trenton on infantile paralysis, proposed an annual March of Dimes dance on January 30—President Roosevelt's birthday—that was accepted by most Newark schools. (pp. 8–9)

In *Remembrance of Things Past*, Marcel Proust writes a sentence that lingers for eight pages; Victor Hugo uses a sentence of over 800 words in *Les Misérables* to help give a sense of urgency and momentum to a particular scene.

Try to write a very long sentence as a class. Pick a topic such as, "Let's write a sentence about trying to cram for a test the night before." Solicit suggestions from the class and write them on the board or a transparency, so they can see how clauses and phrases can be used to elaborate and extend an idea.

Tell students to write two sentences of at least 128 words. The exercise works best if students write about whatever is on their minds at the moment: power relationships at school, a secret desire, a sporting event, walking around the mall, or growing up.

After they have written one or two sentences, have students read them aloud. When they are finished, ask them to identify the specific techniques they used to elongate the sentence, including the phrases, gerunds, conjunctions, and other devices.

An eighth-grade student wrote an eloquent sentence of 158 words: "Last year in seventh grade, when we were only babes, new to the school and new to almost everything about life around here, I felt like my friends would stick with me through good and bad, boyfriends and arguments, jealousy and anger, all those stupid, stuck-up Barbie cliques, and weird, embarrassing situations, but now that eighth grade is here, everything seems so different because friends who were my tightest of amigos way back then seem like strangers now as they walk the halls with cold, zombie eyes, looking right past me as if I were some alien creature who is so ugly and perverted that no one in their right mind would want to hang with me and it makes me sad, real sad, to think that just yesterday, there we were, huddled together during lunch, trying to survive, exchanging sandwiches and gossip, with no one to save us and no one to protect us except each other."

Enrichment

A nice follow-up to The 128-Word Sentence is to have students alter sentence structure again. Have them trade papers and rewrite the 128-word sentences of their peers into at least seven distinct sentences. Both creating the 128-word sentence and transferring lengthy sentences into shorter ones are particularly appropriate for building fluency among students who may be struggling writers or whose primary language is not English.

RESOURCES
Faulkner, W. (1987). "A rose for Emily." In G.F. Waller, K. McCormick, & L.J. Fowler (Eds.), *The Lexington introduction to literature: Reading and responding to texts* (p. 258). Lexington, MA: D.C. Heath.
Roth, P. (2004). *The plot against America*. New York: Houghton Mifflin.

Symbols to Motifs

Type of Activity
Individual

Approximate Time
Two or three 50-minute class periods

Objective
Students will use symbols to create meaning and theme within a creative story. Students will demonstrate the use of motifs within a creative narrative.

Summary
With my Creative Writing and AP English classes, this is the story that most students will send in for publication. In the last 10 years, I've had over 50 students published professionally, and most have come from stories that seek to create meaning through the use of symbolism.

However, while the motif story works very well with the advanced and more motivated students, it has also worked well for me with kids who are not typically considered to be strong in English. In such a case, it becomes more about the expectations. Obviously, I expect stories that are publishable or near publishable from the advanced students, but it is also surprising how well the typical class of 10th graders will do with such an assignment. It is a great critical thinking activity for them and will help add voice and tone to their writing.

The sample in Figure 2 was written by an 11th grader who selected the violin as her motif. She is a good student and was in my creative writing class when she wrote this. It was by far her best writing of the year. This particular piece of writing is from the second paragraph, where the violin first appears, and a page later where it appears a second time. Throughout the entire eight-page story, the violin appears six times and comes to represent the character's fear of abandonment.

Figure 2. An 11th Grader's Motif Writing

A shiver ran through her system as the guitar strumming melded with a violin solo, and her eyes snapped open. The front paws of the wooden chair hit the ground with a thud and suddenly she wasn't alone, the blinding lights and laughter of a late-night bar overpowering the meandering remains of the soulless tune.... She exhaled a tearful gasp of air and took them carefully and turned to face him, and for a moment their eyes met, his worried and caring, hers lost and frightened, and then she heard the last notes of a violin solo and she was gone again, gasping as the door was unlocked, the key was placed in the ignition, and the car was started. And then she left. She left him there in the parking lot, her headlights flashing across his stone face, her purse still forgotten on the floor, and the fading notes of a violin playing in the background.

Materials

Pen and paper, or computer, and copies of the Symbolism to Motifs handout (see p. 31)

Setup

A good setup for this assignment is the Imaging Metaphors lesson (see p. 63) and The Moody House activity (see p. 140). It is recommended that you review definitions for *symbolism* and *motif*, as it will help the students understand the expectations for this assignment.

Procedure

Instruct students to prepare for an extended writing assignment. Motifs should be discussed, pointing out examples of any you might think of. Give the students the following brief instructions, along with the Symbolism to Motifs handout:

> Your task is to create a story that uses one of the following symbols as a motif. The story should be written with a specific tone in mind, and the symbol should recur throughout the story. The idea is for the symbol to become the larger theme of the story. Please do not write a story about your symbol, but instead use the symbol to give depth to your story.

Once you give the handout to the students, offer them the choice of any of the five symbols (or a sixth that you approve) to use in their stories. Ask them to write a story wherein the symbol they select recurs throughout. As with any motif, it is meant to give meaning to the narrative.

As a starting point, ask the students to brainstorm for a bit and come up with ideas as to what their symbol could mean. Typically, the students will struggle some, but once they grasp the idea, they do well. Help with ideas by suggesting that their symbol could represent something intangible like feelings of loss or memories of youth. The concrete for the students is that their symbol should become a theme. This seems to help many of them with the assignment.

Students should be given one or two class periods to work on their stories. Peer critiques are helpful before final revision. With the completion of the stories, many students will wish to read their stories aloud. If time will not allow all students to read their stories, ask the students to prepare a scene from their stories where they felt they did their best writing and read those aloud. This gives everyone a chance to share a part of their story and generates enough interest that the students will often read stories from their peers on their own.

Enrichment

A good follow-up for this assignment is to create a self-assessment rubric for the students. This will most likely be one of the better pieces of writing the students will have done, so the self-assessment allows them a chance to point out those areas where they might have been attempting something meaningful. As teachers, we do not always get what a student might have been trying to do or say, so the self-assessment allows them that opportunity to tell us.

SYMBOLISM TO MOTIFS

Your task is to create a story that uses one of the following symbols as a motif. The story should be written with a specific tone in mind, and the symbol should recur throughout the story. The idea is for the symbol to become the larger theme of the story. Please do not write a story about your symbol, but instead use the symbol to give depth to your story.

Choice of symbols (motifs) that must recur within your stories (choose one):

1. A strong and constant wind

2. A fallen tree

3. A red kite

4. A fiddle or violin (This can be the sound only.)

5. A light mist, almost foglike

6. Create your own: _____ (must be approved by the teacher)

Guidelines:

1. All stories must use the symbol as a motif—something with a deeper meaning to give the story some depth.

2. All stories should seek to find and create depth within the recurring symbol.

3. All stories must incorporate the use of descriptive tone—create a mood through description that recurs and helps add depth to your symbol.

From *Going Bohemian: How to Teach Writing Like You Mean It* (2nd edition) by Lawrence Baines & Anthony Kunkel. Copyright 2010 International Reading Association.

The Delicate Art of Sarcasm

Type of Activity
Individual

Approximate Time
One or two 50-minute class periods

Objective
Students will learn how to use sarcasm effectively in writing.

Summary
A 16-year-old once wrote in an essay for class, "In high school, sarcasm is God." Although somewhat overstated (I actually think popularity and desirability are the deified attributes), the point is that sarcasm is a currency with which adolescents are intimately familiar. Students live and breathe sarcasm every day, yet most use it clumsily and ineffectively. They murmur epithets about "your mama" and make attempts at sarcasm that are mean-spirited and bereft of wit, humor, and logic. Sarcasm used ineffectively or with harmful intent inevitably reflects poorly on the speaker/writer, but sarcasm used effectively can cause an immediate sea change in sentiment about an issue.

When considering the power of sarcasm, I think of Ronald Reagan challenging incumbent President Jimmy Carter for the presidency in 1980 by saying, "There you go again," in response to one of Carter's sophisticated, complex responses. Reagan's intelligent use of sarcasm undermined Carter's legitimacy and helped Reagan win the presidency against a well-liked, incumbent president.

Materials
Print works by writers who write with tasteful, sarcastic wit.

Setup
Have selections from a wide variety of writers who use sarcasm, such as P.J. O'Rourke (almost every piece of writing), Ralph Wiley (most pieces),

Dave Eggers (some pieces), William Buckley (some pieces), literary critic John Simon (some pieces), and film critic Roger Ebert (who indulges in sarcasm infrequently, but is masterly when he does). Comedians such as Chris Rock, Robin Williams, and the late Rodney Dangerfield use sarcasm frequently, although not always in ways that are suitable for classroom use. Choose wisely. Sarcasm can be a devastating rhetorical tool, but you will not be able to teach it if you offend half of your class in the process.

Procedure

Students silently read a selection from P.J. O'Rourke (2007) on growing up in Toledo, Ohio. Then, the selection is read aloud. Ask students to identify where sarcasm is used effectively in the piece and underline the appropriate passages, for example, in the first paragraph:

> I grew up in Toledo, if up is the word. Northwest Ohio is flat. There isn't much up. The land is so flat that a child from Toledo is under the impression that the direction hills go is down. Sledding is done from street level into creek beds and road cuts. In Toledo people grow out—out to the suburbs, out to the parts of America where the economy is more vigorous, and, all too often, out to a 48-inch waistband. But no Toledoan would ever say that he or she had "out-grown" Toledo. We are too level-headed for that.

Explain to students that one brand of sarcasm comes from playing with words and twisting them to new meanings, as O'Rourke demonstrates later in the passage with phrases such as "there isn't much up" and "people grow out—out to the suburbs...out to a 48-inch waistband." Perhaps the most common use of sarcasm is in connection with overgeneralization. O'Rourke overgeneralizes in several places later in this essay—claiming "there is no horizon in Toledo," that no one ever teased a friend about his German name ("Don Eggenschwiler"), and that everyone in Toledo owns "above-ground pools, riding lawnmowers and golf clubs." Obviously, none of those statements are true, but O'Rourke writes them to make a point about the "feel" of the city.

Understatement is another instrument in the sarcasm toolkit. In act 3, scene 1 of Shakespeare's play *Romeo and Juliet*, when Mercutio is slain by Tibalt, Mercutio says, "Ay, ay, a scratch, a scratch; marry, 'tis enough," although he is mortally wounded. As he is dying, Mercutio utters, "No, 'tis

Figure 3. Student Writing About Grand Junction, Colorado

I grew up in Grand Junction, where the desert meets the mountains. Colorado is half mountains; the other half consists of roads leading to mountains. Snow often blankets the peaks surrounding the city, though it rarely snows in town. The land is so arid that most plants stay permanently wilted all year. There is probably some grass in Grand Junction somewhere, though it exists mostly in surreal patches of green on golf courses, which are continually irrigated, and look conspicuously out of place. In Grand Junction, everyone is an athlete—golf, baseball, track, mountain biking, hiking, skiing—though no one makes a big deal out of it. A resident of Grand Junction would never say, "I am an athlete," though they might enter a marathon on Friday, kayak on Saturday, mountain bike on Sunday, and ski on Monday. It is normal to play around outdoors; it is weird to stay inside.

The scenery of Grand Junction is more beautiful than New Hampshire and more exotic than Hawaii but without the attitude or tourist traps. After years of living in crowded, polluted cities where the rain never stops, newcomers to Grand Junction may think the city has nothing to offer and they are right. Grand Junction has no crowds, no pollution, and few rainy days.

not so deep as a well, nor so wide as a church door; but 'tis enough, 'twill serve. Ask for me tomorrow, and you shall find me a grave man."

The Delicate Art of Sarcasm is most effective when you define the boundaries of the playing field. Fair game are politics, current events, popular culture, local interest, cities, hometowns, and school policies. Off limits are teachers, students, family, neighborhoods, and religions. After some discussion of the key points of effective sarcasm, have students write a sarcastic essay about their hometown using the train of thought provided by O'Rourke. Figure 3 shows a piece written by a student from Grand Junction, Colorado.

Enrichment

Have students take a serious subject—a political speech, an essay, or a dialogue from a book—and improve it using sarcasm and understatement. Instruct them to replace stodgy and ineffective phrasing with sharp-edged and purposeful wording.

RESOURCE

O'Rourke, P.J. (2007, April 13). Why it's good to come from nowhere. *Toledo Free Press*. Retrieved December 1, 2009, from pjorourkeonline.blogspot.com/2007/04/why-its-good-to-come-from-nowhere.html

Secrets

Type of Activity
Individual

Approximate Time
Two 50-minute periods of writing

Objective
Students will indirectly describe a secret (or secrets) between two persons, using subtleties of dialogue, setting, and tone. This exercise is particularly useful in getting students to write with subtlety and wit.

Summary
Although Secrets seems a bit complicated at first, some of the best writing I have ever received from students has been the result of this activity. Furthermore, Secrets seems to help students understand the power of understatement and implication and seems to transfer well to students' nonfiction writing.

Materials
Pen and paper, and copies of the Secrets handout (see p. 37)

Setup
Have students read and discuss O. Henry's (1906) short story "The Gift of the Magi." Emphasize that O. Henry does not simply reveal what happens in the story, but that he allows the actions and dialogue of the characters to illuminate the secrets, the characters' fears, and each character's feelings about the other.

Pick the two most theatrical students in class and ask one to read Character A (female) and the other to read Character B (male). Do not allow the students to see each other's scenario. Ask the two students to have an impromptu 5- to 10-minute conversation in character in front of the class.

Procedure

Discuss "The Gift of the Magi."

Tell the class that they are about to witness a scene in which each of the characters has a secret that he or she is hiding from the other. Ask the class to note how the two characters interact—the dialogue, facial reactions, and gestures—as the two students act out their conversation. At the end of the skit, discuss the ways that silence and awkwardness can imply meaning. Have students guess at each character's secret, then have characters A and B reveal them. Discuss the ways in which the characters implied and the other students inferred their secrets.

Now ask students to write a short dialogue between two persons, in which at least one has a secret. The idea is to make the writer write through implication and indirect description.

Enrichment

Once students have written their stories, ask them to form groups of three or four. Students should read each group member's story, decide which would make the best short play, and vote on it. Then, two students act out the scenario and the writer directs. If a video camera is available, the fourth student (or the writer) films. If no camera is available, then the fourth student acts as the critic. Eventually the story is turned in and the play is performed for the class (or the film is shown).

RESOURCE
Henry, O. (1906). *The gift of the magi*. Retrieved February 11, 2010, from
    www.gutenberg.org/dirs/etext05/magi10h.htm

SECRETS: LEARNING TO WRITE WHAT ISN'T THERE

Character A (female):

You have just been nominated for an internship as an artist-in-residence at *Le Louvre* (famous art museum in Paris, France). You are best friends with B, who has on more than one occasion come through for you. Recently, you have found that B has developed some severe problems with gambling. B has told you that some men have been looking for him lately to collect gambling debts he owes. You have repeatedly lectured B on his gambling, but you suspect that he continues to gamble away every cent he earns. You are uncertain what course to take about yourself and your relationship with B. You wonder if you should seize the opportunity to go on the art internship or devote yourself to helping rehabilitate B during this critical time. Of course, B would not want you to forego a career opportunity just to help him. You need to find out if B is still gambling and how B might react to the possibility of you leaving the country.

Character B (male):

You have just won $4 million in the state lottery. You wonder if you should tell A, who used to be your best friend, because she has been acting very strangely lately, and you do not understand why. A seems to have everything going for her, but A has repeatedly criticized you for gambling too much. True, you spend way too much of your paycheck on silly long shots, but now your gambling has finally paid off. You are not sure if A still wants to be your friend, and you fear that revealing that you have just won $4 million will perhaps push her into being your friend just because of the money. You want a *real* friendship, not one based on money. A few weeks ago, your family decided to go to Ireland this summer for three weeks. You considered asking A to go with you and your family, but now you think that you would rather not invite A if she is going to act like your guard dog. You would still like to be A's friend, but you need some time to think about being a millionaire, too. In this conversation with A, you want to find out why she has been acting so strangely and if she really likes you for who you are. You have to decide today whether or not you want A to go to Ireland with you and your family. Perhaps it might be best simply not to mention the trip at all.

The Guts:
Fundamentals of Writing

*What the young writer needs to do, of course, is study
sentences, consciously experiment with them, since he can
see for himself what the difficulty is, and can see for himself
when he has beaten it: Where variety is lacking, sentences
all run to the same length, carry over and over the same old
rhythms, and have the same boring structure.*

From *The Art of Fiction: Notes on Craft for Young Writers* by John Gardner

You live in a time of educational reform. Your classes have become
increasingly standardized. Although you haven't been given a script
for teaching, you have been given a calendar that is closely aligned
to the pages within the textbook you are expected to use. Excited to begin
the year and knowing that you'll do what's expected, and perhaps a little
more, you ask your students to write a short essay that will demonstrate
their creativity and writing skills.

Michael, the 14-year-old boy whose feet seem to get in the way of his
every step, walks rather hesitantly toward your desk. He's holding his
rough draft of the essay he is doing for this initial writing sample. As he
hands it to you, he lingers a moment, watching you closely, then sort of
blurts out that he really doesn't know what to write about. It's obvious to
you that he's proud of what he's done, but nervous that you'll point out its
flaws. You nod, smile, and begin reading his draft. It doesn't take long to
realize that there is no punctuation. Michael is trying not to look nervous
as he watches you. You start over, trying to think of something nice to say.

As you read Michael's essay, you wonder, where do you begin teaching
writing? He's in the ninth grade and should know how to write a sentence.
Because this is the first writing sample for the class, you worry about how

many more of these kids cannot write a complete sentence. The textbook that they'll be using begins with verb agreements, tense shifts, then compound and complex sentences. This assumes the students are writing at a level that is well beyond the sample you've received from Michael.

Should you back up, create your own lesson to explain the difference between a fragment and a run-on sentence? You hand back the draft to Michael without shattering his feelings and begin to sort through the papers from the class. Over and over, you see fragments, run-ons, and a serious weakness in basic sentence structure. The few students who are actually writing complete sentences seem very content writing nothing more daring than a simple subject–verb pattern. You realize that at this level, you're going to need to back up quite a bit simply to reach a starting point where you can begin working on some basics.

You had hoped to try some new ideas with this class, but the things you had in mind require a fundamental understanding of sentences. Now, with an increasing sense of dread, you begin to wonder how much time you'll need to spend going over what should have been learned in elementary and middle school. What you really need is to engage your students to their maximum potential, to find an unconventional way of creating a basic understanding of sentences.

You make a decision: If you're expected to be successful teaching the skill sets proposed within the textbook, you will need to bring the students up to speed. You know your department chair to be a by-the-book person, but she has also been teaching long enough that she understands a purposeful adjustment to the expected curriculum when she sees it. To cover yourself in the event of a surprise visit, you send her a quick e-mail informing her that you'll need to do some remediation before the required lessons from the book.

The truth is that if things go well, you may be able to simply skip some of the dreariness found within the text. You've spent many days marveling at the apathy that takes over when the students are told to work out of their books. You remember your own classes and the difference between an exciting lesson and book work. Their response seems as automatic as yours used to be. Many students do nothing; some do the work quickly, and then do nothing. There is little interaction, and often there is little learning taking place. It's time to try something new, time to rattle some cages, time to make sentence structure intellectually stimulating and—dare you think it—fun.

Repetition and Parallelism

Type of Activity
Individual

Approximate Time
One 50-minute class period

Objective
Students will learn about the effectiveness of repetition and how to compose parallel sentence structures that lead to rhythmic, powerful cadences in oral and written language.

Summary
Repetition and parallelism are tools of writers and speechmakers that are rarely mentioned in secondary schools. An unfortunate oversight because these tools are foundational rhetorical devices, which once learned, will never be forgotten. An unfortunate oversight because repetition and parallelism add elegance and rhythm to composition. An unfortunate oversight because errors in repetition and parallelism abound in academic and popular publications.

    Repetition and Parallelism is somewhat more sophisticated than many exercises in this book, as it relates to rhythm and rhetoric, which are usually considered secondary to meaning and pronunciation among remedial and English-language learners. Nevertheless, these techniques are essential and can be easily learned, even by students who have minimal reading comprehension skills.

Materials
Video and text of the presidential inauguration speech by President Barack Obama (2009; see Resource section) and copies of the Excerpt From President Barack Obama's Inaugural Address handout (see p. 45)

Setup

Students view a video of the inauguration speech by President Obama.

Procedure

After students view President Obama's inauguration speech, hand out the text of the last part of the speech. Note to students how many gifted speakers use repetition to accentuate certain points. Show students how President Obama uses repetition in the second and third paragraphs of the excerpt with the word *new* ("Our challenges may be new. The instruments with which we meet them may be new.... What is required of us now is a new era of responsibility"). Have students scour the text of the speech and highlight words that show up again and again. Discuss with students the most popular words in the excerpt and speculate why President Obama repeated these particular words. List the most common words on the board.

Play the video of the excerpt of the speech again. When President Obama repeats a word, have students raise their hands.

Of course, not only words but also sentence structures can be repeated. Go through the speech again as a class, pointing out how President Obama uses parallel sentence structures. In the first part of the excerpt, the phrase "It is the" introduces many sentences. Explain to students that when a writer wants to emphasize the end part of the sentence, he or she might begin the first part with weak words, such as "It is." President Obama continues with his emphasis on the end part of sentences when he uses "What is" and "This is" as parallel structures later in the speech, and finally "Let it be told" and "Let it be said."

At one point, also note how President Obama juxtaposes several terms in sequence: "honesty and hard work, courage and fair play, tolerance and curiosity, loyalty and patriotism." There is a rhythm in listing pairs of terms. He does not list honesty, thrift, and hard work, because the word *thrift* would ruin the cadence.

Have students highlight repeated phrases in a different color from the repeated words. Play the excerpt from President Obama again. This time, when President Obama uses a repeated phrase, students stand up.

Finally, note to students that to begin sentences with "It is," "This is," or "What is" is actually weak writing style. In contrast, one of the most

Figure 4. A Student's Revised Version of Portions of President Barack Obama's Inaugural Address to Demonstrate Repetition and Parallelism

Being an American brings with it responsibilities. Being an American means listening to God as we shape our uncertain destiny together. Being an American means that we cherish our liberty and our creed. Being an American means that men and women and children of every race and every faith can join as one in celebration across this magnificent mall. Being an American means a child whose father less than 60 years ago might not have been served in a local restaurant can stand before you today to take a most sacred oath.

memorable repetitions is Martin Luther King's "I Have a Dream" speech. The refrain "I have a dream" provides much more power than "It is." Ask, for instance, How could President Obama have changed his wording to make his speech more effective? Figure 4 shows a student's passage in which "This is" has been replaced as a repetitive device with "Being an American."

Enrichment

As with any political speech, President Obama's inaugural address is also useful for analyzing other rhetorical techniques, such as citing an authority, President George Washington, at the end of the speech, aligning with the listener/reader by using the pronouns *we* and *us* and the possessive pronoun *our*, and making allusions to implicitly narrative structures in passages, such as

1. The kindness to take in a stranger when the levees break
2. The selflessness of workers who would rather cut their hours than see a friend lose their job
3. The firefighter's courage to storm a stairway filled with smoke
4. A parent's willingness to nurture a child

In example 1, the mention of "when the levees break" is reminiscent of stories of courage shown by residents of New Orleans in the aftermath of Hurricane Katrina. In example 2, the narrative is about an altruistic worker who takes a salary cut to keep a friend employed. Examples 3 and 4 refer to stereotypical feel-good stories with which we are all familiar: the fireman ignoring peril to save a life, and the parent whose love alone propels a child to greatness. Direct identification and discussion of some of these narrative structures.

RESOURCE

Obama, B.H. (2009, January 21). *President Barack Obama's inaugural address* [Speech]. Retrieved December 19, 2009, from www.whitehouse.gov/the-press-office/president-barack-obamas-inaugural-address

EXCERPT FROM PRESIDENT BARACK OBAMA'S INAUGURAL ADDRESS

<u>Speech delivered January 21, 2009:</u>

For as much as government can do, and must do, it is ultimately the faith and determination of the American people upon which this nation relies. It is the kindness to take in a stranger when the levees break, the selflessness of workers who would rather cut their hours than see a friend lose their job which sees us through our darkest hours. It is the firefighter's courage to storm a stairway filled with smoke, but also a parent's willingness to nurture a child that finally decides our fate.

Our challenges may be new. The instruments with which we meet them may be new. But those values upon which our success depends—honesty and hard work, courage and fair play, tolerance and curiosity, loyalty and patriotism—these things are old. These things are true. They have been the quiet force of progress throughout our history.

What is demanded, then, is a return to these truths. What is required of us now is a new era of responsibility—a recognition on the part of every American that we have duties to ourselves, our nation and the world; duties that we do not grudgingly accept, but rather seize gladly, firm in the knowledge that there is nothing so satisfying to the spirit, so defining of our character than giving our all to a difficult task.

This is the price and the promise of citizenship. This is the source of our confidence— the knowledge that God calls on us to shape an uncertain destiny. This is the meaning of our liberty and our creed, why men and women and children of every race and every faith can join in celebration across this magnificent mall; and why a man whose father less than 60 years ago might not have been served in a local restaurant can now stand before you to take a most sacred oath.

So let us mark this day with remembrance of who we are and how far we have traveled. In the year of America's birth, in the coldest of months, a small band of patriots huddled by dying campfires on the shores of an icy river. The capital was abandoned. The enemy was advancing. The snow was stained with blood. At the moment when the outcome of our revolution was most in doubt, the father of our nation ordered these words to be read to the people:

"Let it be told to the future world...that in the depth of winter, when nothing but hope and virtue could survive...that the city and the country, alarmed at one common danger, came forth to meet [it]."

America: In the face of our common dangers, in this winter of our hardship, let us remember these timeless words. With hope and virtue, let us brave once more the icy currents, and endure what storms may come. Let it be said by our children's children that when we were tested we refused to let this journey end, that we did not turn back nor did we falter; and with eyes fixed on the horizon and God's grace upon us, we carried forth that great gift of freedom and delivered it safely to future generations.

Excerpted from *President Barack Obama's Inaugural Address* [Speech], B.H. Obama, January 21, 2009, retrieved December 19, 2009, from www.whitehouse.gov/the-press-office/president-barack-obamas-inaugural-address.

Combine and Count: Sentence Combining With a Twist

Type of Activity
Individual and group

Approximate Time
One 50-minute class period

Objective
Students will combine and rearrange simple sentences into grammatically correct compound and complex sentences.

Summary
Sentence combining has been around for a long, long time, but I don't see a lot of teachers using it these days. Perhaps with standardization and testing becoming so prevalent, there is too little time. Still, sentence combining can be a fun way to work on sentence-level skills. Combine and Count brings a fresh angle to an old idea.

    When I run Combine and Count through my class, I find hands are constantly being raised. The students like the puzzle approach and show impatience when they do not get the answer right away. Often, students will revise a sentence five or six times, resulting in an environment reminiscent of a good writers' workshop. Of course, you can create your own puzzles.

Materials
Pen or pencil and copies of the Sentence Combining handout (see pp. 49–50)

Setup
Little setup is needed for this assignment. A discussion on the various sentence types is sometimes helpful for the students. For such a

discussion, the three types of sentences they will be working on are simple (independent, subject–verb), compound (two independent sentences joined by conjunction), and complex (independent with dependent clauses joined by subordinating conjunctions).

Procedure

Give students the Sentence Combining handout. To make the lesson more engaging, have the entire class work on sentence sets one at a time. On the first one, it helps to have the first person come up with a grammatically correct combination, give a word count, and then place that count on the board. When another student has a lower word count for a grammatically correct sentence, change the count on the board.

The first set of sentences is the easiest, so students will solve it quickly. The second and third sets, though, require some rearranging to make them work. These will have students arriving at different solutions. Students will often write run-on sentences, and in such cases, you need to inform them that it's a run-on and help them work out a comma and conjunction, or rewording.

When the students have been working for a bit on the second or third set, write the count for your solution on the board and ask them to try to match it. For the fourth set, I usually end up writing the word *Marco's* on the board and then tell the students that that is how they may want to begin their sentence. This will quickly solve the problems many of them are having.

The solutions I have used for each of the examples on the handout are as follows. Please note that you should always be open to the idea that a student may find a better solution, in which case that will become the best solution.

1. A shy tattoo artist had wild designs on a dancer who worked at the Polar Club in Kodiak, Alaska. (19 words)

2a. With his large, broom-carrying mother chasing him, the boy ran quickly into the house and tripped over his dog. (20 words)

2b. Because his large, broom-carrying mother was chasing him, the boy ran quickly into the house and tripped over his dog. (21 words—is this one better?)

3. The monkey doing the macarena in the window looked at the woman who walked slowly past. (16 words)

4. Marco's rare gift of eating massive quantities of watermelon without getting sick has allowed him to win contests throughout the state. (21 words)

Enrichment

For enrichment, do a reverse activity of sentence combining. Basically, ask the students to uncombine a series of large run-on sentences. This is another form of sentence work that reinforces revision and grammar skills, especially work on commas. The Sentence Uncombining handout (see p. 51) is the set of sentences I use that students seem to have enjoyed working on the most. For this activity, I don't ask for word counts, but instead have the students read their solutions aloud, and I have the other students offer better solutions. I also work with the students on these and offer my solutions. More than once, I've had a student show me up on some of my created sets.

Here is my solution for the first set. I'll leave the other solutions to the capable readers of this lesson plan.

Boggy Swamp has attracted and delighted monsters since the beginning of time. To allow these creatures the full benefits of the swamp, slime, mud, and sacrificial maidens have been provided. As a result, these silly monsters can vacation, feast, and sun themselves almost any time of the year.

SENTENCE COMBINING

Combine each of these sets of sentences into one sentence that sounds good and is grammatically correct. It is possible that there could be more than one correct combination, but the goal is to find the combination that uses the fewest words. You must keep all of the information in the finished sentence. When you think you have the correct combination, count your words and write the number in the space provided.

Set 1:
A tattoo artist had designs.
The artist was shy.
The designs were wild.
The designs were on a dancer.
The dancer worked at the Polar Club.
The Polar Club was in Kodiak.
Kodiak is a city in Alaska.

Your new sentence: _____

_____

_____

Total words: _____

Set 2:
The boy ran.
He ran quickly.
He ran into the house.
His mother was chasing him.
His mother is large.
She is carrying a broom.
The boy tripped.
He tripped over his dog.

Your new sentence: _____

_____

_____

Total words: _____

(continued)

SENTENCE COMBINING (*continued*)

Set 3:

The woman walked.

She walked slowly.

She walked past a window.

There was a monkey in the window.

He was doing the macarena.

He looked at the woman.

Your new sentence: _____

_____

_____

Total words: _____

Set 4:

Marco can eat massive quantities of watermelon.

It's a rare gift he has.

This gift has allowed him to win contests throughout the state.

He never gets sick when he eats watermelon.

Your new sentence: _____

_____

_____

Total words: _____ (The best correct combination has 21 words.)

SENTENCE UNCOMBINING

Uncombine the sentences into several simple sentences that make sense, are sequenced correctly, and are grammatically correct.

Set 1:

Boggy swamp has attracted and delighted monsters since the beginning of time to allow these creatures the full benefits of the swamp slime mud and sacrificial maidens have been provided and as a result silly monsters can vacation feast and sun themselves almost any time of the year.

_____

_____

_____

_____

Set 2:

I like to eat grasshoppers smothered in chocolate when I eat them I like to savor their sweet and tangy flavor but once in awhile I like eat them fast so they crunch loudly and my mother says I shouldn't eat disgusting things but I eat them anyway because I like to eat them we never seem to have enough bait when we go fishing and I know the fish like to eat grasshoppers also so I'm like a fish.

_____

_____

_____

_____

Set 3:

I remember the time I became a frog and it was depressing as everybody knows as frogs can never get the good dates so maybe the flies don't taste that bad it is not mall food which I like sometimes until I became green because I'm a frog.

_____

_____

_____

_____

From *Going Bohemian: How to Teach Writing Like You Mean It* (2nd edition) by Lawrence Baines & Anthony Kunkel. Copyright 2010 International Reading Association.

Show-Me Sentences

Type of Activity
Individual

Approximate Time
One 50-minute class period

Objective
Students will revise sentences to incorporate imagery, tone, and sensory writing.

Summary
For quite a few years, I have been telling my students to "show me" within their writing. Some have gotten it, but many have not. Typically, students will momentarily improve a passage or two that they have written to get me off their backs, but they seem to forget all about show-me writing by their very next paper.

A few years ago, I began creating "telling sentences" and placing them on the board for the students to rewrite into "showing" scenes. This simple device has turned out to be amazingly effective, and doing several of the sentences together with the class has helped them grasp the idea that they can write descriptively as a matter of course. More often, show-me writing starts showing up in papers without me having to scream about it. This little technique seems to work.

Materials
Pen and copies of the Show-Me Sentences handout (see p. 55)

Setup
Provide each student with a Show-Me Sentences handout.

Procedure

Discuss with the class the idea of "showing" instead of "telling" within their writing.

Provide each student with a Show-Me Sentences handout and talk them through the directions. On the handout is a column of sentences that tell the scene or moment. Next to these are spaces for the students to re-create the scene or moment, showing or writing them more descriptively. There is an example at the top of the columns that is helpful for the students. Inform them that they may rewrite the scene into several sentences, but they should work on incorporating visual and sensory images to show the reader the scene they are rewriting.

After the students have worked through the various telling sentences, and hopefully created some interesting scenes, ask for volunteers to read their recreations aloud. It is sometimes helpful to point out to the students when they have used imagery or senses within their writing. Praising specific techniques will go a long way toward creating a memorable lesson for the students on descriptive writing. Figure 5 presents a few examples of students' show-me sentences.

Figure 5. Students' Show-Me Sentences

Telling: The girl stood on the corner of the busy intersection and witnessed the accident as it happened.
Showing: The toes of her tiny pink shoes were placed on the tip of the gum-encrusted curb when a chauvinistic Corvette raced by and ran the red light, crashing into a large truck brimming with rocks as it crawled through the intersection.

Telling: The hunted creature ran through the thick forest and screamed as the thorns cut into his skin.
Showing: Dribbling and panting, the creature had nowhere to hide. By instinct, the beast ran for foliage to escape the predators. The trees and roses that had once been his home grabbed his flesh and tore muscle from bone as he cried out in anguish.

Telling: The boy pulled a large fish out of the river.
Showing: His small palm launched into the flowing river, splashing drops of water on his focused face. His knees damp and dirty from the riverbank, he dragged a fish his own size back home.

Enrichment

With some practice, you can use the Show-Me Sentences activity fairly early in the year to set things up for several follow-up opportunities within students' writing. For example, my 10th graders are required to write descriptive narratives that discuss an event or philosophy. Once they have finished a draft and completed a peer review session, I ask them to find three single sentences from different paragraphs within their narratives. I have them write each sentence on a separate piece of paper with room for several sentences below each. Once they have their sentences written, they are asked to turn those into show-me sentences. They know the phrase *show-me* from the earlier activity and, more often than not, will create some nice descriptive writing from these sentences. These show-me sentences are then rewritten into the narratives as part of the revision process.

When I first began teaching show-me sentences, I was working with ninth graders at a rural high school in north Florida. The school had incorporated a semester-long writing class in the hopes of raising ninth graders' scores on the Florida standardized writing test. Figure 6 gives some show-me samples from those ninth-grade students. The assignment was a character story with descriptive writing. The samples are from students who were not strong writers, and it is a different type of revision for them. Grammatically they still need work, and there are some spelling errors, but the difference in their description and effort is worth noting.

Figure 6. Ninth-Grade Students' Show-Me Sentence Revisions From Descriptive Writing Pieces

---

Tim
Show-me 1: He layed there, thinking of the day ahead.
Revised show-me: The tired old man delicately layed on a sea of cotton and springs. He pondered, trying desperatly to determine what he would accomplish today.

Casey
Show-me 3: He arrived at the theater and was seated.
Revised show-me: He cautiously parked his truck as close as was possible and sat quietly for a moment. He took a deep breathe and exited his car and made his way toward the musical. A young flashy girl lead him to his seat, nerveoulsly smacking her gum while she walked.

SHOW-ME SENTENCES

In the rows below, there are two blocks: one containing a telling sentence and one for rewriting that sentence into a descriptive scene that "shows." Please note example A and make your best attempt to rewrite each "telling" sentence into a sentence, or several sentences, that show the scene. Think of word choice and using senses (smell, touch, sight, taste, sound) to create something good. Feel free to invent details within the descriptions.

Telling	Showing
Example A: The old man stood in the grass and relaxed as the sun went down.	Example A: He felt the grass beneath his feet and a smile softened his eyes. A gentle breeze whispered against his wrinkled skin as the sky paled yellow, then to a deep crimson, and within a breath it became night.
The boy pulled a large fish out of the river.	
The girl stood on the corner of the busy intersection and witnessed the accident as it happened.	
The woman had a terrible headache.	
The meadow slowly came to life as the sun came up.	
The hunted creature ran through the thick forest and screamed as the thorns cut into his skin.	

From *Going Bohemian: How to Teach Writing Like You Mean It* (2nd edition) by Lawrence Baines & Anthony Kunkel. Copyright 2010 International Reading Association.

Hide the Adjective

Type of Activity
Group

Approximate Time
One 50-minute class period

Objective
Students will identify adjectives and use them in writing, learn to use descriptive adjectives in sentences, use and increase listening skills through active engagement, and learn creative sentence structure and writing techniques.

Summary
Instantly, students will recognize the need to seek out and use words that they otherwise would not have attempted. It will quickly become evident that not only are students enjoying themselves and beginning to take more pride in their written products, but also they are producing writing that is more sophisticated.

   This activity is equally effective for teaching nouns, adverbs, verbs, prepositional phrases, adverbial phrases, and other parts of speech. Hide the Adjective is an activity that can be used to teach not only adjectives but also a variety of skills across the curriculum. For a 50-minute class of 25 students, it is recommended that 20 minutes be left for reading the stories.

Materials
Index cards or small slips of paper big enough to hold a written word (and definition if no dictionaries are available)

Setup
One adjective will be needed for each student in the class. It is best to select colorful and interesting adjectives to bring forth some colorful and interesting sentences. For instance, the word *gargantuan* would probably

produce a more colorful sentence than the word *big*. On each slip of paper, write one adjective (and its definition, if no dictionary is available).

Procedure

After a brief discussion of adjectives, give each student one of the slips of paper containing an adjective. It is important to explain to the students ahead of time that if any of their classmates see their adjective, one point could be taken from them. Once students have their adjective in hand, hidden from all eyes, instruct them to write a half-page story using their adjective somewhere in that story.

Before the stories are written, inform the students that their stories will be read aloud by the teacher, and the class will be given three attempts to guess the adjective that was assigned for that particular story. Their adjective should be circled or underlined in the story. The object is for writers to be as creative as possible and try to hide their adjective within the story, which means they will need to use other adjectives as often as possible.

Only one adjective per sentence is allowed, so each student should strive to use as creative an adjective as possible at every opportunity. Once students begin listening to the stories being read, many will immediately wish they had used better adjectives, which opens the activity to unlimited possibilities for the next time it's used.

Assessment

Applying a grade to this activity is ultimately up to you. It has been effective to use points as extra credit, which not only gives the students motivation and instant feedback but also allows the teacher the opportunity to give points or a grade as each story is read aloud. Points are scored two ways. First, when a student raises his hand and correctly guesses his peer's adjective, he receives 1 point. Second, if no one guesses an adjective within three tries, the writer of that story receives 1 point.

To keep the same students from getting all of the points, it is recommended that you call on different students whenever possible and that each student be allowed a maximum amount of points possible (usually 3 guessing points plus 1 point for successfully hiding their adjective).

Enrichment

Block off a week for this activity and begin with something simple like Hide the Noun. After doing this activity once, most students realize that they could have done a better job hiding their word and look forward to playing again. The next day, follow up with Hide the Adjective, and the results will be pleasantly surprising. Not only will the students do a much better job at hiding their word, but also the level of their writing will increase, and the stories will become more entertaining.

By the end of the week, most students will have become adept at listening and using creative sentences to mask what would otherwise be an obvious word or phrase. The engagement of the students to write creatively while targeting specific skills, and the repetition of listening, identifying, and repeating these target words, has proven to be more effective for retention than any grammar book on the market.

Scrambled Sentences

Type of Activity
Individual or group

Approximate Time
Half of a 50-minute class period (15–25 minutes)

Objective
Students will use their knowledge of paragraph organization, sentence structure, logic, and the use of transitions to assemble a group of sentences into a cohesive paragraph.

Summary
Scrambled Sentences is a short but very useful activity that requires students to consider transitions, context clues, and sentence rhythm.

Materials
Pen and paper, or computer, and copies of the Scrambled Sentences handout (see p. 61)

Setup
Write the following words on the board: "Ready, fire! Aim."

Ask students what is wrong with this sequence of words. Discuss the importance of ordering information. Ask students for examples of bad organization.

Procedure
Distribute the Scrambled Sentences handout and ask students to rearrange the sentences into a coherent and comprehensible paragraph. Tell students to use as many context clues as possible. Give them a time limit of 10 to 15 minutes and monitor their progress.

After they have completed the rearranging, ask the students to share their responses. Inevitably, students will differ on their ordering of the sentences. Ask students to defend their ordering with reference to specific context clues and logical flow of content.

Once students have shared and a consensus of opinion is reached, hand out the Scrambled Sentences: Actual Passage handout (see p. 62). Compare the actual passage to the consensus opinion of sentence sequence and get individual opinions. Discuss the similarities or differences and try to explain the rationale for the writer's decisions.

Enrichment

The next step is to have students use one of their own paragraphs as fodder for scrambling. Once a student scrambles his sentences, he can exchange papers with a peer. As above, the peer attempts to order the sentences into a paragraph. When the student's guess at order is compared against the actual writing, often the writer realizes that his composition lacks a sense of logical progression and internal context clues. As a result, this activity can sometimes substantially enrich the overall quality of student writing.

SCRAMBLED SENTENCES

Order the following sentences so that they make the best sense:

1. "If God had come to you seventeen years ago and said, 'I'll make you a bargain. I'll give you a beautiful, wonderful, happy and healthy kid for seventeen years, and then I'll take him away,'" Tim said, "you would have made that deal in a second."

2. He knew that, he said, and then argued, almost persuasively, how the tree was to blame.

3. He hit a tree the day he got his license.

4. Yet his friend Tim Russert of NBC called Friday, devastated as we all are, and said the only thing that has helped.

5. As a parent, you live in fear your child will die in a car wreck, and in his year and a half of driving Christopher did manage to wreck all four of our family cars.

6. We just didn't know the terms.

7. But it was a sudden, initial attack of juvenile diabetes that killed him, despite medical heroics and fervid prayers.

8. "It wasn't my fault, Dad."

9. And last spring he backed one of my cars into another of my cars, which must be a record of sorts.

10. And that was the deal.

11. It is awful and horrible and sad, and no words can comfort his four grandparents, his brother and sister, his friends or his parents.

12. He announced his other accident to me over the phone by beginning, "Dad, you know those air bags stink when they go off."

13. "Well, Christopher," I said, "it was yours or the tree's."

Adapted from "My Son, a Gentle Giant, Dies," by M. Gartner, in E.J. Farrell & J.E. Miller, Jr. (Eds.), *The Perceptive I: A Personal Reader and Writer*, 1997, Lincolnwood, IL: National Textbook, pp. 173–174.

SCRAMBLED SENTENCES: ACTUAL PASSAGE

Excerpt from "My Son, a Gentle Giant, Dies" by Michael Gartner:

As a parent, you live in fear your child will die in a car wreck, and in his year and a half of driving Christopher did manage to wreck all four of our family cars. He hit a tree the day he got his license. ("It wasn't my fault, Dad." "Well, Christopher," I said, "it was yours or the tree's." He knew that, he said, and then argued, almost persuasively, how the tree was to blame.) And last spring he backed one of my cars into another of my cars, which must be a record of sorts. He announced his other accident to me over the phone by beginning, "Dad, you know those air bags stink when they go off."

But it was a sudden, initial attack of juvenile diabetes that killed him, despite medical heroics and fervid prayers. It is awful and horrible and sad, and no words can comfort his four grandparents, his brother and sister, his friends or his parents.

Yet his friend Tim Russert of NBC called Friday, devastated as we all are, and said the only thing that has helped.

"If God had come to you seventeen years ago and said, 'I'll make you a bargain. I'll give you a beautiful, wonderful, happy and healthy kid for seventeen years, and then I'll take him away," Tim said, "you would have made that deal in a second."

And that was the deal.

We just didn't know the terms.

Excerpted from "My Son, a Gentle Giant, Dies," by M. Gartner, in E.J. Farrell & J.E. Miller, Jr. (Eds.), *The Perceptive I: A Personal Reader and Writer*, 1997, Lincolnwood, IL: National Textbook, pp. 173–174.

Imaging Metaphors

Type of Activity
Individual or group

Approximate Time
One 50-minute class period

Objective
Students will discuss the use of images as vehicles for symbolic and metaphorical writing, learn creative writing techniques, and use images in their writing to create symbolism and metaphors.

Summary
Students enjoy Imaging Metaphors and will produce some wonderful writing and discussion. I created this lesson as a prereading activity for the Crossing Edson's Bridge lesson (see p. 177), but have found it to be useful as a prepoetry activity as well.

Materials
Index cards or slips of paper with selected images written on them (An example of suggested images is provided in Step 2 of the Procedure section.)

Setup
The class should be divided into groups of two or three, unless the activity is being assigned individually.

Procedure

Step 1
Introduce the activity with a short discussion on imagery in writing and how various images can be used in writing to create symbolism and metaphors, eliciting and giving examples when possible.

Step 2

Give each group (or individual) an index card containing one written image. Below are some suggested images that may prove effective:

- A rusty swing set
- An abandoned factory
- An abandoned garden
- A single rose
- A broken doll
- A sudden thunderstorm

Once all groups have received their cards, instruct them to discuss the image they have been given and create a short piece of writing of approximately one page, using their image as symbolically as possible. This image is to become the central metaphor of whatever it is they are writing. Students may write an essay, a short piece of fiction, or a poem—the only requirement is that the writing must be as metaphorical as possible.

Step 3

Once all groups have finished creating metaphors from their images, oral presentations will ensue. Each group should explain what their image was intended to represent and how they chose to make it so.

Enrichment

Using this lesson prior to Crossing Edson's Bridge (see p. 177) is a great setup for a unit on reading comprehension and figurative language within selected readings.

Literature and Nonfiction: Connecting Writing to Reading

Literature was written to make an impact. Readers must talk about the literature, argue about it, look for points of agreement and disagreement with the author, look for ways it connects to their lives. We must keep this at the heart of what we do in the literature class and find ways to value and evaluate the meaning our students make through literature.

From *Exploring and Teaching the English Language Arts*
by Stephen Tchudi & Diana Mitchell

You decided to become an English teacher only after you worked at many other jobs: real estate sales, fry cook, retail manager, bartender, banker, baker, and computer geek. You made more money in other fields, but you always wound up missing the books. As a teacher of English, you get paid to read and think. Not a lot of money, of course, but in no other profession would it be important to know why the caged bird sings, who Big Brother really is, or the significance of a the letter *A* displayed in a scarlet hue. But this year your students seem less motivated to read than ever. So you've made it a habit of perusing bookstores on a regular basis.

You cruise for hours along the aisles of the megastores that are part of a national bookstore chain, intermittently sipping your cup of coffee and exploring for books. At the neighborhood used-book store, you burrow for books amid the live-in cats and discarded stacks of romance novels, all the time rationalizing that you can buy twice as many books as you ordinarily would because of the discounted prices. You buy books from Amazon, of course, because you put everything on your credit card with one click. You hate Amazon's "book recommendations for you" blurbs that keep showing up when you sign in, but then again, you have ordered several recommended books, and a few have turned out to be jewels.

In short, you are a book junkie. You have enough books at home in your to-be-read pile that it would be impossible to finish them all within a single lifetime. You want to share your love of books with your students and help instill in them a yearning to read and learn. But you won't be able to do that by simply asking them to open their books and begin reading. You need to get them interested first. Sometimes you read passages to your students from the book you are currently reading at home. You want them to know good writing when they hear it, and you want them to feel the same kind of rush that you did when you came upon a book that stirred your soul.

You know your students have options—now more than ever. They can choose among hundreds of cable television stations, thousands of video games, millions of websites. When the lights go out, parents retire to sleep, and no one is around to monitor what happens next; you wonder if your students will have the temerity to ignore the television, walk past the video games, and overlook the computer. As an English teacher, you hope that your students have books hidden under their pillows, stacked in their closets, and stuffed into the dry corners of the bathroom.

Turning students into real readers and deep thinkers is perhaps the greatest challenge of the 21st century. A student who reads voraciously and attempts to engage the mind before leaping into action (or conclusions) is going to flourish. In contrast, a student who struggles with reading and fails to engage the mind before leaping into action faces exponential challenges.

You make sure that reading materials are plentiful, contemporary, and eclectic, and you discuss great books, interesting articles, and superb student writing at every chance. One truth is incontrovertible: Students can write only as well as they can read.

Mystery Bags

Type of Activity
Group

Approximate Time
Works best over two 50-minute class periods

Objective
Students will learn how to construct suspense effectively and gain an appreciation of the genre of detective fiction.

Summary
Mystery Bags enlivens the study of detective fiction. Especially for those who seem to have some difficulty getting started, Mystery Bags effectively promotes students' storytelling potential.

Materials
Have as many bags for clues as you need for each group of 3 or 4 students (6 to 8 bags for a class of 24 students). Gather together objects that might be found at the scene of a crime, such as a note, scissors, a ticket stub, a key, or a bottle. Put 6 to 14 unique objects in each bag.

Setup
Divide your class into groups of three or four students. Show them an excerpt from a film depicting the adventures of Sherlock Holmes, in which Holmes and Watson attempt to deduce the significance of certain clues.

Have students read Sir Arthur Conan Doyle's "The Adventures of the Blue Carbuncle" or *The Hound of the Baskervilles*, John Clifford Mortimer's *Rumpole á la Carte*, or a short story by Raymond Chandler. Discuss with students the techniques the authors use to build suspense and how sleuths use their powers of deduction to solve crimes.

Figure 7. A Student's Mystery Bags Writing

An umbrella, still wet with the late night icy drops, is in a puddle near the door. On the table lies the rough draft of an article, face-up, still paper-clipped with a few stray pencil marks of indecision in the margins. The deceased preferred to edit with a pencil.

Her limp body was still warm with no signs of a physical struggle or any evident wound. No liquid around the desk, no bottle of wine, no sign of poison. A torn ticket stub to a movie theater on the East Side was on the floor near her foot.

Jumbo enters the scene in his trademark moth-eaten old football letter jacket, and he picks up the torn ticket stub. The digital clock has been knocked to the ground and is blinking an infinite repetition of 2:52. Flashing, flashing—too easy.

Jumbo's wet hair, plaid shirt, and three-day growth of whiskers make him look as if he might be one of the homeless along Washington Avenue, but the uniforms on duty stay out of his way as he wanders about the room. He plays with a rubber band with his fingers and wears a pencil behind his left ear. He looks down at the table and picks up an envelope that had been torn carefully down the side. Opening the letter, he reads the first sentence: "Congratulations! Your article on human rights in China has been accepted for publication in *International Trade Quarterly*." Next to the letter is an empty disk case, but no sign of a disk.

Procedure

Discuss how Sherlock Holmes (or the detective from the film clip and novels you used) solved crimes.

Tell students that a crime has been committed and they must use their powers of deduction to piece the clues together. From the available evidence, every group should decide these facts:

- The crime
- The victim
- The perpetrator
- The sleuth (must have a name, some readily apparent physical features, and distinctive tastes)
- Obstacles to solving the crime

From this, students should write collaboratively within their groups a mystery story that uses these components, as demonstrated in Figure 7.

Enrichment

An obvious next step is for students to perform, audiotape, or videotape their stories.

A Playlist for Holden: A Unique Approach to Character Analysis

Type of Activity
Individual

Approximate Time
Will vary from one 50-minute class period to several, depending how much of the project becomes out-of-class work

Objective
Students will analyze a character in literature through dialogue, plot events, and conflict and resolution.

Summary
When I first came up with this playlist assignment, I thought I was on to something very original. A short amount of research showed me that I was not the only teacher with this idea. There are many variations available on the Internet, but I like the clarity that A Playlist for Holden offers. A Playlist for Holden is the favorite activity of many of my students. Music and playlists are a huge part of their day-to-day lives, and asking them to think of a character as a kind of peer seems to give a sense of authenticity to the project.

This lesson will be most effective if the students have read a novel focused on a primary character (or characters). This lesson uses J.D. Salinger's novel *The Catcher in the Rye* and the character of Holden Caulfield. *The Catcher in the Rye* is a universally recognized novel with an iconic primary character, but the assignment would be equally effective with any character from almost any novel.

Assessing this assignment is a little different. There is the written portion of the project, which almost ends up being secondary to what the students typically have to offer with regard to their insight into the character they have written about. In short, if the requirements are met, it becomes very much about the content of what they've said as opposed to the quality of the writing they've done.

I use presentations for the students to discuss their playlists. I don't play all of the songs—in fact, typically I don't play any of them—but instead have the students explain the lyrics and their reasoning. This is typically an enjoyable class for the students, as they are all interested in each other's musical selections. Music is a language that most of them speak. Indeed, during these presentations, the discussion becomes very much about Holden, and students inevitably make observations that are insightful and sometimes unexpected.

Materials

Pen and paper, an MP3 player, a computer with Internet access and iTunes, or a music list with lyrics, and copies of the Playlist for Holden handout (see p. 72) (Students will need access to several songs and their lyrics.)

Setup

Distribute the Playlist for Holden handout.

Procedure

Once the students have finished the novels or stories they have been reading, you should create competing statements with regard to the primary character (or characters) that the students may be divided on. For example, using *The Catcher in the Rye*, you could write the following two statements on the board:

1. Holden Caulfield is an insightful, wise adolescent who points out and analyzes many of the flaws of our society.
2. Holden Caulfield is more hypocritical than insightful. He says one thing and then does another, relying on cynicism or sarcasm in addressing the flaws of society.

Ask students to think about each statement and decide which they agree with most. Students then take out a sheet of paper and create a short list of reasons why they, personally, agree with the statement they chose. Next, ask them to write the statement that they chose along with a list of scenes from the book that they remember that might support their reasons. Once students have written their rationales and identified scenes from the book to support their ideas, group the students based on which statement they selected (groups of three or four work well) and have them compare their lists of reasons and scenes.

This is a good introduction to the project, as it allows students a chance to develop individual opinions of Holden, as well as to think of the moments within the novel that may have created those opinions. Once students discuss their feelings about Holden with students who have similar thoughts, and you are comfortable with their understanding, move on to the bigger project.

After students move back to their original seats, give them the Playlist for Holden handout, then give them a minute to read over the instructions. When the students begin looking up and raising their hands, go over the handout to clarify your expectations. Depending on whether you will be allowing them time to work on these in class or requiring them to work on these as homework, it's important to also discuss time and due dates. Typically, the first step will have the students begin brainstorming for the songs they may wish to use.

Enrichment

A project like this is an excellent opportunity to reach those students who may learn, or express themselves, a bit differently. Although most of the students will enjoy the opportunity to think about a book in terms of the music they listen to, not all students are going to be full of enthusiasm. Some are just more visual, and the playlist idea will not be the best opportunity for them to interpret or analyze a character within a novel.

It is for these students that you might want to offer a second option for analyzing Holden. On page 73, you'll find the Graphic Novel or Comic Book for Holden reproducible for an alternative assignment that you could give with the playlist project; this option allows more artistic students to use their skills to re-create the story in a comic book or graphic novel format.

PLAYLIST FOR HOLDEN

The playlist:

Make a 10-song mixed playlist or CD for Holden Caulfield as if he were around today. With this project, there are also two written assignments:

1. In a letter to Holden, explain why you are including each of the 10 songs on the playlist or CD. This should be a page of writing that tells him something about the song and why you thought it would be good for him.

2. Each song should have a paragraph description telling Holden why he will like it—an explanation of the rationale as to why you thought the song was a good choice. In each paragraph, connect lyrics from the song to scenes and situations from *The Catcher in the Rye*. In other words, tie the song lyrics to Holden and the events in the book.

Requirements:

• A written playlist of 10 songs (artist and song title) on CD (If this is not possible, a copy of the lyrics from each song may be used.)

• A letter to Holden

• One written paragraph per song, giving a rationale for each song choice

From *Going Bohemian: How to Teach Writing Like You Mean It* (2nd edition) by Lawrence Baines & Anthony Kunkel.
Copyright 2010 International Reading Association.

GRAPHIC NOVEL OR COMIC BOOK FOR HOLDEN

Instructions:

With regard to Holden's character, choose the most important scenes—in your view—and tell Holden's story of *The Catcher in the Rye*. The quality of your project will be determined by the following:

• The extent to which your graphic novel or comic book portrays Holden's character throughout the entire novel

• The quality/effort put into the artwork

• A written introduction and summary in which you explain what you tried to capture in your recreation of the novel (e.g., "I wanted to emphasize the extent to which Holden rejects society and reveals himself as a rebel in the American spirit. I did this because...and showed it by..."): This must be analytical in nature and discuss insights into Holden's character that go beyond simple statements of fact and opinion.

Note:

If you select this project instead of the playlist, be aware that you are expected to produce an equivalent amount of writing and thought.

Philosophy in Short: A Video Project on Existentialism

Type of Activity
Group

Approximate Time
Four 50-minute class periods

Objective
Students will demonstrate an understanding of a specific universal theme and philosophy commonly found within selected works of literature.

Summary
I had been using book trailers in my class for a couple years when I thought of applying the idea to a theme or philosophy instead of a book. A philosophy trailer is similar to a movie trailer, but a movie trailer already has images to work with, such as movie posters and clips from films. With a philosophy trailer, the creator has to convert the ideas into images that will generate interest. I thought of attempting a book trailer for Albert Camus's *The Stranger*, but somehow I imagined that as falling short; existentialism is difficult enough to ask the students to grasp. Indeed, the best trailers I could imagine would have been those that sold the idea of absurdism or existentialism more so than the book.

That was the birth of this assignment, which asks students to demonstrate an understanding of the themes and ideas within the book. Some of the students struggle a bit at first, but after my first time doing this project, I had a selection of both shorts and trailers as examples that set the bar exactly where I wanted it—very high. Figure 8 shows some posters that came with the trailers students created in my class.

Figure 8. Students' Philosophy Trailer Posters

Materials

A video camera or camera capable of video, copies of the Philosophy in Short handout (see p. 78), and a computer with Internet access, video-editing software, and a word-processing program

Setup

This lesson works nicely after having the students read both Camus's *The Stranger* and R.K. Narayan's *The Guide. The Stranger* is an essential book with regard to existentialism, and *The Guide* offers a nice contrast to *The Stranger.* While I use this lesson to teach and assess student understanding of existential philosophies, other teachers have begun using it for themes such as the hero's journey and morality in John Steinbeck's novels and good versus evil in Harper Lee's *To Kill a Mockingbird.* For explanation purposes, the lesson included here focuses on existentialism.

Before jumping in to the lesson, students should read *The Stranger* and *The Guide,* although it could work as a lesson for any novel.

Procedure

As a class, discuss at length the theme within the novels, then give the students the Philosophy in Short handout and explain the assignment.

After the students have looked over the instructions, allow them the opportunity to organize themselves into groups of no more than four. (I find this works well with seniors, but with 10th graders or lower, you might want to determine the groupings.) Once all questions have been answered and the students have grouped themselves, allow the class the rest of the period to organize and plan. Then, allow the next period for the students to film, organize, and do whatever they need to get ready; you might want to time this activity so that the students will have a weekend to finish the projects.

The following class is for presentations. These are usually a treat, and when the students are given the chance to explain what they've done, the discussions are rich in demonstrating an understanding of the philosophy.

Enrichment

Try an Ebert and Roeper (or Siskel and Ebert for those of us older teachers) follow-up to the presentations. Begin the assignment with a viewing of the Ebert and Roeper show, noting to the students how they argue about some of the movies and become nitpicky at times. Then, pair students and give each pair a selection of student-created trailers and shorts, with a list of criteria to look for. (These criteria could come from the handout that was given with the original assignment.)

Instead of a simple peer review, the students should prepare a review presentation, either via video or in front of the class. This is a nice venue for providing feedback on the trailers and shorts, not to mention a good way of having the students analyze the videos for the philosophy you are targeting.

PHILOSOPHY IN SHORT

<u>There are two tasks to complete:</u>

1. Create a philosophy trailer that sells or markets the idea of existentialism as it relates to the common themes within both *The Stranger* and *The Guide*. Think of such themes as individualism, fate, community, and choices. Think of the themes mentioned as they pertain to the novels. A philosophy trailer is similar to a movie trailer, but a movie trailer already has visual images to work with, such as movie posters and clips from films. With a philosophy trailer, the maker (your group) has to convert the ideas into visual images that will generate interest. The trick is to convey a sense of what the philosophy is about while promoting both of the novels as works that are fundamental to these philosophies.

    Another option for this task is the creation of a short film that is existential and addresses the themes mentioned previously. If you choose to do this option, your group should attempt to have allusions of references to the novels, whether within the dialogue or as juxtaposed text with images. Like the prior task, the idea is to convey a sense of what the philosophy is about, while working in the novels as fundamental to the philosophy.

    Here's what must become part of your trailer:

    - An introduction to the concept of existentialism
    - An attempt to address the themes of individualism, community, fate, and choices
    - Use of the two novels as foundations for the philosophy and the video

    Most trailers of this sort run about 3 to 7 minutes long, and so should yours.

2. Create a movie-style poster on the computer to go with your trailer; if a computer is unavailable, a hand-drawn poster will work just as well. Look to the theaters to get a sense of what this should look like and how big it should be.

Author Cards

Type of Activity
Individual

Approximate Time
One or two 50-minute class periods

Objective
Students will do research on a particular author, write a brief summary of the author's life, consider the author's themes, compare the author's themes against their own beliefs, and write a poem intertwining the author's life and works with their own values and accomplishments.

Summary
Too often in English, the curriculum is so packed with required readings that a student rarely gets a chance to dive deeper into one particular author's works. Author Cards provides a platform in which students can think deeply about an author and a body of works. Author Cards moves students out of the dullness of the superficial ("What color was his hat?") and into the realm of the existential ("In what ways am I enthralled and repulsed by Poe?").

The combination of art (abstract drawing), sound (recording of recitation by a professional actor), poem (literary dialogue response poem), citation (favorite passage), and précis (life and works of the author) helps provide a more complex, complete portrait of an author than does the traditional approach of silent reading and answering questions. Furthermore, after completing the exercise, which should take about the same amount of time as the traditional approach, students will have an idea about their true feelings about an author's literary works.

Materials
Several works by a single author

For this example, Edgar Allan Poe will serve as the author of interest. Poe's works might include the poems "The Silence," "The Raven," and "Annabel Lee," and the short stories "The Fall of the House of Usher," "The Tell-Tale Heart," and "The Silence" (Poe wrote both a poem and a short story with this same title). Borrow, buy, or download a copy of *Closed on Account of Rabies* (1997), a truly bizarre CD that features a host of actors and singers reciting the stories and poetry of Poe. You will need a CD player, art supplies (paint and paper), scanners, computers equipped with publishing software such as Microsoft Publisher or the free software Scribd, and copies of the Author Card Assessment handout (see p. 83).

Setup

Students should have read several poems and stories by a single author prior to this activity. Keep in mind that Poe is only one example, as Author Cards can be done with any author.

Procedure

Students research the life and times of Edgar Allan Poe, using biographies, textbooks, and websites, then write a short summary of his life in their own words.

Play "The Raven," as voiced by Christopher Walken on *Closed on Account of Rabies* (1997, CD 1, track 2). As Walken recites the poem, students paint an abstract image inspired by the poem. You will need to encourage students to make the painting abstract. They will be tempted to draw moons, gravestones, and birds flying across the sun, but advocate against any representational art. Have them attempt to paint in concert with the reading of the poem.

Let the paintings dry, then scan them.

Give students a copy of the Author Card Assessment handout and explain the assignment. Have them choose their favorite passage by Poe. The favorite passage and abstract painting will take up the front page of the card.

Students write a "critical commentary" on any one of Poe's works, in which they examine themes, major characters, point of view, tone, language, and plot. The critical commentary will serve as the back page of the card. Using the computer will allow students to type this right into the software program.

Students write a short biography of Poe's life and works for page 2. Again, the computer will allow students to type the short biography right onto the page. Have students save their work.

Students provide an image of Poe and an image of themselves for page 3, which will also contain an original literary dialogue response poem penned by students based on prompts the teacher calls out, to which students respond in writing. For example, the following is the list of prompts I developed for studying Poe:

Line 1: Your interpretation of a favorite line from one of Poe's works in your own words

Line 2: Your response to the sentiment expressed by Poe in line 1

Line 3: The opposite meaning, in your own words, of a line you find compelling in Poe's work after you've figured out what his line means

Line 4: Aspects of Poe that you dislike most or find most upsetting

Line 5: An analogy of Poe's life that includes an action word (verb)

Line 6: An analogy for your own life that includes an action word (verb)

Line 7: A description of the real Poe

Line 8: How you are different from Poe

Line 9: What you and Poe share in common

Most prompts ask students to assess the themes and life of Poe in light of their own lives. Although the idea of a literary dialogue response poem may seem strange, inevitably students will compose some incredible verse. The format of the poem forces students to consider the author in new and different ways. Figure 9 shows an example of what a finished author card might look like.

Enrichment

Author Cards is infinitely adaptable to whatever needs a teacher or student might have. For example, a teacher of English-language learners might encourage those students to create a poem in their native language on page 2 of the author card, with an accompanying translation on page 3.

RESOURCE
Willner, H. (Producer). (1997). *Closed on account of rabies: Poems and tales of Edgar Allan Poe* [CD]. New York: Mercury/Universal.

Figure 9. A Student's Poe Author Card

"Were I called on the define, very briefly, the term Art, I should call it "the reproduction of what the Senses perceive in Nature through the veil of the soul." Edgar Alan Poe

I have never been sure what to think about Edgar Allan Poe. For me, his stories are as intriguing as they are revolting. While his prose is beautiful, many of his subjects are grotesque and disquieting—a man is buried alive, a murderer mercilessly kills then goes insane, a beautiful young woman dies needlessly, a lonesome man visited by a bird goes crazy, Poe's plotlines are similar in their projections of tragedy and their dark, inevitable hopelessness.

With both a mother and a father who were actors, it almost seems as if the young Edgar was destined at birth to become an artist. His father deserted the family shortly after Edgar was born and his mother died shortly afterwards. Edgar was taken in by a businessman named Allan (giving Poe his middle name), though he was never formally adopted by the Allan family. In fact, after Edgar failed at being a soldier and was court-martialed out of the army, his foster father cut off relations. Edgar eventually married his 13-year old cousin Virginia when he was 29. Although they lived twelve years together, and were happy by most reports, Virginia became sick with tuberculosis and died a slow, painful death when she was only in her twenties.

In many ways, Poe is the stereotypical artist, poor and starving, but also brilliant. Today, literary critics hail Poe as "the first real American writer," "the first writer of detective fiction" ("The Murders in the Rue Morgue"), "the first writer of science fiction" (*The Narrative of Arthur Gordon Pym of Nantucket*) "the father of Romanticism" ("Annabel Lee") "the first writer of horror fiction" ("The Pit and the Pendulum") ad infinitum. When reading Poe, it is only natural to wonder if his descriptions of death, dying, torture, misery, and grief are inspired by his own, true-life events.

Poem for Edgar

Certain, empty headed visions of commonplace
gods
Anxious to destroy, hesitant to build
The soul retreats into resignation
Endless misery and pain, and the suffering,
always the suffering

Fear seduces, will not abate
Clawing through jungle with fragile fingers
Rage of desire, the utter brutality of real life
To kiss the sorrows of the world

I aspire, but Poe creates.

"The Silence" begins with a conversation between "a demon" and the narrator. The demon tells the narrator about a "dreary region" in Libya, near the Zaire River where "the waters of the river have a saffron and sickly hue—and they flow not onwards to the sea, but palpitate forever and forever beneath the red eye of the sun with a tumultuous and convulsive motion." The demon refers to the place as a kind of heaven, though the description makes it sound more like hell. Poe even manages to make the flowers in this place seem ghastly—"at the roots strange poisonous flowers lie writhing in perturbed slumber."

The narrator sees a grey rock that displays the text DESOLATION on it. Later, a man in a toga, reminiscent of a senator from ancient Rome, shows up and is described as having "the features of a Deity." The Roman looks lost and forlorn and trembles "in the solitude." Then, a thunderstorm rolls through, producing flash floods, lightning, gusts, and broken trees.

In response to the storm, the narrator curses "the river, and the lilies, and the wind, and the forest, and the heaven, and the thunder, and the sighs of the water-lilies" and, as a result, the storm dissipates. After everything gets quiet, the grey rock changes its text message from DESOLATION to SILENCE and the Roman shudders and flees in terror.

The original title of this short story was "Siope—A Fable: In the manner of the psychological autobiographies" but has also been known as "The Shadow" and "The Silence." Some literary critics have noted that Poe might be satirizing popular psychological autobiographies of the time, but there is little apparent humor in the story. The story begins in desolation, and while that makes both the narrator and the Roman uncomfortable, desolation seems superior to no stimulation at all. The terror of "The Silence" is silence, itself.

AUTHOR CARD ASSESSMENT

<u>Each of the following is worth 20%:</u>

1. Front page: The abstract painting completed during the reading of "The Raven" and a favorite passage by Poe from any of his works

2. Page 2: A short summary of the life and works of Poe

3. Page 3: Your literary dialogue response poem, an image of Poe, and an image of you

4. Back page: Critical commentary on a specific work by Poe and your name

5. Overall quality of writing and aesthetics

Imagining Transcendentalism: A Video Essay Project

Type of Activity
Individual and group

Approximate Time
Four 50-minute class periods

Objective
Students will analyze and identify transcendentalist philosophies and authors within various works of the Romantic era in American literature. Students will create imagery for, and from, written works and incorporate photography, filming, and video editing into a product that juxtaposes writing with images.

Summary
While the video essay requires delving into technology, I have continually been inspired by the products I get from students. I've taught the video essay at schools with little to no resources available and at schools with an abundance of resources, yet in either case, the final products were similar in quality.

This is the type of assignment in which visual learners will excel. Often, some of the most amazing products will come from the students who typically show the least engagement during class. Ultimately, with this project, the students also will demonstrate an empathetic level of understanding with regard to what has been taught. The project works well as an assessment of how well students understand both the philosophy and the authors of the period.

Materials

A video camera or camera capable of video, copies of the Requirements for Transcendental Video Essays handout (see p. 89), and a computer with Internet access and a word-processing program

Setup

Although this project is based on philosophies within American literature of the Romantic period, it is easily applicable and adaptable to any philosophy or period within literature (or life).

Procedure

Imagining Transcendentalism is based on the Conduct of Life activity (Baines & Kunkel, 2002). Once students have read and discussed several works by transcendental authors, such as Ralph Waldo Emerson and Henry David Thoreau, and Romantic authors, such as Walt Whitman and Charles Dickens, instruct them to create a personal narrative that attempts to discuss how the philosophy of transcendentalism is, or is not, relevant to their own philosophies on life and the world in which they live. Make available the works of several authors and ask the students to incorporate at least two author quotes that help them say what they are trying to say with regard to transcendentalism. Typically, one class period is necessary to complete these narratives.

After completing their narratives, students are grouped by three or four and asked to read one another's narratives, highlighting any areas where they might have written similar thoughts or ideas in their own essays.

Once the students have read all of the narratives within their groups, tell them that they will be creating a nonverbal group video essay that incorporates the writing from each of their essays with quotes from transcendental authors, music, and images. With these instructions, give the students the Requirements for Transcendental Video Essays handout. It is helpful to have samples of video essays to show the class, but on the first run, that is not always possible. Figure 10 shows some images taken from several student video essays.

Figure 10. Images From Student Video Essays

Once the students have been given the assignment and expectations, it is helpful to spend some time discussing the video-editing process. Today, all computers come standard with a video-editing program— Windows comes with Movie Maker, and Macs have iMovie. For most students, it will be as easy as a PowerPoint presentation once they play with the program. The most difficult part of the assignment for many will be getting the footage from the camera to the computer. Still, today's students are very tech savvy, and I have yet to have a group not finish the project due to technical difficulties.

When all questions have been answered, give students the period to begin arranging their ideas and plan a film. It is helpful if they are told to write a list of all quotations they will use within their videos. This also allows you to be certain that they have combined their essays and found appropriate passages. It helps to make the due date fall after a weekend, as that will give students the time needed to finish and edit the film. When all videos are due and complete, spend a class period watching the products that were made.

Enrichment

A nice follow-up for the video essay is to have the students turn the video into an actual essay. The idea is for them to consider the visual nature of the essay they first turned into a video and see if they can now write a descriptive piece that captures the images of the video. I've done this several times and found the level of writing to be significantly higher than the initial essays that began the project.

Some students will begin to write about their video, but I attempt to stop that and guide them into an essay that simply describes *images* with connections to the philosophy. For example, where one student may begin writing, "Our video uses Emerson...," I will redirect that essay into the description of the scene that was attached to the quote they are thinking of, with a transition into the quote.

Recently, a 10th grader wrote in her introduction to the original essay, "I have always had this idea of what you see is what you get...." The essay that was written after her video had a similar introduction, but it is much more developed:

Don't worry about the rest of the world swirling around you, they have their own problems to deal with. You have the rain, soil, and sunshine to nurture you. With society's pressures, though, what you see may not be what you get.

It is interesting that not only is the writing much more graphic, but also there is a change in what she says, almost a shift or clarification of her thoughts on the topic. In this way, what began as an individual writing assignment morphs into film, then back into words. The results will, more often than not, be surprising.

RESOURCE
Baines, L., & Kunkel, A. (2002). *Teaching adolescents to write: The unsubtle art of naked teaching* (pp. 117–148). Boston: Allyn & Bacon.

REQUIREMENTS FOR TRANSCENDENTAL VIDEO ESSAYS

<u>Your group video essay must include:</u>

• Opening and closing credits

• Two or more quotes from each group member's essay

• Two quotes per group member from different transcendental authors/people

• Video images or scenes that capture the essence of all group members' quotes and essays

• A creative group still

• Music or sounds that fit the images of the video

• No narration or talking

The length should be the approximate time of a song, which seems to work well for this project. You may use a variety of songs or music, but it is recommended that you find the perfect song and go with that.

From *Going Bohemian: How to Teach Writing Like You Mean It* (2nd edition) by Lawrence Baines & Anthony Kunkel. Copyright 2010 International Reading Association.

Samuel's Satire: Board Games and Mark Twain

Type of Activity
Individual and group

Approximate Time
Three 50-minute class periods

Objective
Students will analyze and identify satire or other techniques, themes, and treatments in literature.

Summary
I've been doing board games on novels for some time now, but it's only been within the last three years that I've used them for a more focused analysis of the novels. At first I used them for plot, character, and conflict, because asking the students to analyze a novel for theme or technique can present a challenge. It requires the students to find meaning within the plot, characters, and conflict, and I find that many adolescents today are intimidated by this process. I do this lesson now with my sophomores, and what I've found is that they are completely capable of dissecting a book for a targeted theme or technique, as long as they know what it is they are looking for.

This lesson works well for me, because I spend the time talking about and teaching the theme or technique the students are analyzing. I do this as an individual assignment, because I find it difficult to teach reading skills, so this allows me the opportunity to address reading through both plot and analysis. The students have many questions, and many are frustrated at my "no trivia questions allowed" rule, but ultimately, they create games that are insightful and creative. I eliminated trivia from the assignment, because I found that most of those students who didn't wish to do the critical thinking needed for the assignment would resort to creating games in which a player would land on a square and have to answer a question. Those games didn't tell me how well they understood the satire or theme within the book I was using—only that it was there.

Materials

Boards for board games or large poster paper, craft materials or markers and crayons, and copies of the Finding the Satire in Huck handout (see p. 94)

Setup

Before you begin this assignment, students should read a novel or a longer short story, and you should lead a discussion of a particular theme, technique, or form/genre. For this lesson description, I use Mark Twain's *The Adventures of Huckleberry Finn* as the novel, and satire as the technique studied. I have also used this assignment with Kurt Vonnegut's *Fahrenheit 451*, on the theme of dystopia and authority, as well as William Golding's *Lord of the Flies*, on power and symbolism.

Procedure

To help the students focus, ask them to create a plot timeline of the novel. Instruct them to focus on the events of the story in the order that these events are written. It is not necessary for the students to write down every minor happening, but they should be able to bullet out the events that may have some significance. I demonstrate the plot line by drawing a horizontal line on the board and then drawing short, vertical lines off of it. I write the first event of the book above the first vertical line. For example, for *The Adventures of Huckleberry Finn*, you could write, "Tom's gang and the oath." Then, check to make sure the class understands.

Because the focus of the lesson is satire in *The Adventures of Huckleberry Finn*, I tell the students to use the plot line to jot down moments within the book where they think satire may have occurred, then write "satire" below a vertical line to correspond with the event written above. Below "satire," the students should write what this satirical text is mocking. For example, I have "Tom's gang and the oath" above the first vertical line, and beneath it I write, "satire" and "Romanticism." I tell them, "events on top, satire on bottom." We discuss Tom's oath and how it could be Twain's way of making fun of Romanticism.

With the example on the board, give the class enough time to create these plot lines for satire. For the last part of the class, place students in groups of three or four and let them share the events and satires they have found. In the next class period, go over the topics the students have identified as possible satire. Write these topics on the board and discuss the events that are involved in their findings. This typically leads to a good discussion, and the students should demonstrate a focused analysis on the topic you're looking for. Once you have several topics on the board, narrow them down to those that most students have found and use the opportunity to discuss any other moments you may want them to examine more closely.

Figure 11. Students' Satire Board Game

Once all students have a plot line with the satire topics, give them the Finding the Satire in Huck handout. Once the students have been given a moment to read the assignment, go over the details.

Allow the students approximately 20 to 30 minutes to brainstorm and share ideas, and then make it an out-of-class assignment. I have done this in class, though, using poster board and markers, and while the products aren't as artistic, the process is just as impressive. It is helpful to show an example, as in Figure 11, and I always have pictures of previous board games available.

Enrichment

A great follow-up for this assignment is to allow the students a period to play the games. Many will find that their games only take minutes to complete, and some will discover that they have, in fact, created a great game on the book. During the entire game-playing period, though, the students are discussing the novel and the satire within.

FINDING THE SATIRE IN HUCK

Your task is to create a map-based board game that follows Huck and Jim's journey and is primarily based on the satire within *The Adventures of Huckleberry Finn*. You may draw the game on a poster board or create an actual board. All board games must include a map that represents Huck and Jim's adventure. When you are done, there should be an actual game that you and your classmates can play, including pieces, dice, cards, or whatever, as well as instructions and rules of play.

The game should represent the various characters, events, and settings within the book that you found to have some element of satire within the story. The type of game you create is up to you, *but you must attempt to place rewards and penalties throughout the game that are based on the satirical qualities of those characters, events, and settings that you choose to include.*

Effort is important in this task, as is your ability to make sense of (and show the importance of) the satire presented in *The Adventures of Huckleberry Finn*. Your approach to completing this assignment should be to use the timeline you created. From this timeline and the class list of satire within the book, you could decide which scenes would best represent the satire you are seeking to show. Please feel free to be creative.

Following are the criteria for your games:

• Does *not* use trivia or Q&A within the game

• A written overview and explanation of the game that tells how your game incorporates the satire into the game or scoring

• Important characters, settings, and events that tell what is happening and what is being satirized directly on the game board and in the game

• A scoring system that is based on the satire within the book, based on your interpretation of the event

• A knowledge of the book that demonstrates you have kept a plot line and a map and have identified several topics that are being satirized, as well as the topics they are satirizing, within the book

From *Going Bohemian: How to Teach Writing Like You Mean It* (2nd edition) by Lawrence Baines & Anthony Kunkel. Copyright 2010 International Reading Association.

Language: Building Vocabulary

Language is the pliable adhesive that helps to form, identify and bind nations, communities, neighborhoods, groups, societies, and personal relationships. Language is also the means by which those groups give voice to their ideas, dreams, despairs, hopes, fears, memories of yesterday, and visions of tomorrow.

From *Language Exploration and Awareness: A Resource Book for Teachers* by Larry Andrews

You cringe as the supervising teacher points to the 20 vocabulary words on the chalkboard. You saw them when you came in and remembered what it was like being in high school and experiencing those endless lists of vocabulary words. You are not surprised, though, when the students are given the assignment. After all, it's a Monday. "Write them down, take them home, look them up, write a definition, use them in a sentence, and bring them back tomorrow," says the teacher. You wonder who invented this technique as the standard for teaching vocabulary.

As the students turn in their vocabulary assignments the next day, they are handed a test asking them to match definitions to words and words to definitions. You notice that most of them did the homework and acknowledge that most will pass the test, yet you feel relatively certain that few students will remember any of these words beyond next week.

This is the class that you are scheduled to take over in a week—the first time in your student-teaching experience that you'll be teaching alone. Vocabulary to these students is simply one throwaway day per week, part of the gauntlet they must run if they want to pass. The vocabulary words have little meaning to them. They are simply linguistic placebos to be carried for a limited time within their short-term memories.

Flash forward several years. It's a Monday morning, and you smile as the third student of the morning pops his head in the door to look over the scoreboard for Vocab War. This student is part of the winning class, and he pumps his arm in victory before leaving. The student who popped in before him was from the losing class, and you ignored the expletive he whispered when he saw the scores. You know that since he checked, he'll be ready for the quiz later on. You began using Vocab War as your primary method for vocabulary instruction during your student teaching some years ago and are always amused (and a bit amazed) at the level of competition that arises within and between your different classes.

You know the students desperately need to learn words, to learn the value of words, and you also know that most of them don't realize it. Somehow, you need to revitalize the study of language so that students will look forward to learning vocabulary not dread it.

You began this method for vocabulary instruction as an attempt to break away from the traditional method of having students write the words, define them, and then use them in a sentence. Your hope was to have the kids interact with words on a different level—something more memorable. You have tried several fun methods for vocabulary, all successful, but ultimately settled on the method that seemed to fit you and your teaching style.

While you know the students are not learning all the words they are given, you are reasonably certain that they are learning, remembering, and understanding the five words you've selected to work on for each week. Your methods are different, but as the students go forth and talk about the game and the words, no one can dispute your results.

Word Bingo

Type of Activity
Individual

Approximate Time
One 50-minute class period

Objective
Students will increase vocabulary skills, learn and demonstrate dictionary skills, organize and write sentences under time constraints, and use difficult words in context.

Summary
One thing I have found with this game is that students will quickly pick up the proper usage of descriptive words, and their sentences will become colorful and effective even without a complete understanding of a particular word. Most students are intimidated at first by the restricted time limits, but they quickly become motivated once they circle two or three words in a particular column. A small reward works to motivate those students who need a reason to play. I also give the winner of the game an automatic A on the written work if I plan on grading it, which is always an effective motivator for grade-conscious students. If the game ends too quickly, most students will wish to continue for a second- or third-place finish.

Although this is a game I've had a great deal of success with in all of my English classes, I cannot take full credit for this idea. It actually began with three boys in one of my ninth-grade skills classes who wanted to invent a game that would make looking up definitions more fun. I've developed the idea into more work than they originally had intended, but every time we played, they would remind me that the game was their idea. I thank them for the idea—and for their enthusiasm.

Materials
Pen and paper, and a set of dictionaries

Setup

Select 25 level-appropriate vocabulary words and write them in random order on the chalkboard. The following is a sample list of words that I have used with an average ninth-grade class:

timid	foray	boastful	stoical	esteem
antipathy	reverence	pompous	plunder	toady
genial	modest	bleak	pacifier	atonement
vain	ravage	repair	shrew	coy
ardent	enmity	honor	apathetic	zealous

Procedure

Instruct all students to draw a bingo sheet of 25 squares or rectangles (5 columns with 5 rows). It is not necessary for students to put numbers or letters by the columns and rows. Once all students have their bingo sheets ready, instruct them to fill each square on their sheets with one of the words from the chalkboard, in random order. Students may put a word in any square they like, as long as they do not use any word twice; recommend to students that they not copy the words in the order they are written on the board, which will ensure that none of their classmates have the same bingo sheet as them.

After all students have completed their bingo squares, select the first word and call it out; to make the game more ceremonious, I usually write the words on little squares of paper and pull them from a box. Students circle the word that was called on their bingo sheets. They then must look up that word, list its part of speech, and use the word properly in a sentence. Inform students that they will have two minutes to complete this before the next word is called out. This continues until a student completes a column or row of five words and proclaims, "Bingo!"

When the student calls "bingo!" he or she must read each word from the completed bingo column or row, along with the part of speech and the sentence containing that word. If the word is read correctly, the part of speech is right, and the sentence demonstrates the appropriate context for the word, that student has won. If the student incorrectly identifies the part of speech or misuses the word in a sentence, tell him or her how it was misused, as well as the proper use, and explain that that column or row on his or her sheet becomes forfeit. Students can fix their error, though, in case that word becomes part of a different column or row in progress. Then, the game resumes until the next student calls "bingo!"

Enrichment

What has also worked well with Word Bingo is teaching terms and vocabulary that are being taught across the curriculum. For instance, a middle school social studies teacher I know uses this game to teach geographic terms. Students are armed with their textbooks and given words such as *strait, fjord,* and *escarpment.* To the teacher's delight, the students not only begin using the words correctly but also begin to understand the geographic concepts that go with them.

Face Reading

Type of Activity
Individual and group

Approximate Time
Four consecutive days, 10 minutes per day

Objective
Students will learn the meanings of 12 sophisticated adjectives.

Summary
Face Reading is useful not only for teaching new vocabulary but also for expanding students' oral-language skills. After a week of Face Reading, it is guaranteed that the words studied during this exercise will start showing up in students' everyday conversation and academic writing.

    This activity is particularly powerful for remedial readers and English-language learners. The combination of pictorial representation, oral recitation, and repeated writings of the words and definitions significantly enhances word-recognition skills.

Materials
Pen and paper, blank index cards, and copies of the Adjectives for Facial Expressions handout (see p. 102)

Setup
Students study lists of adjectives and their meanings prior to class.

Procedure
Select two of your most dramatically inclined students to illustrate facial expressions. Write an expressive adjective in very large letters on the board. Go over the meaning of the word with the two dramatic students,

Figure 12. Example of a Student's Face Reading Card for Adjectives

Word	Face	Definition
lachrymose	☹	sad
exultant	☺	very happy
disconsolate	☹	cheerless
amiable	☺	friendly

then have them act it out in front of the class. After several seconds of the students acting out the word silently, say a simplified definition. Write " = " and a definition next to the word, as well as a graphic representation of the emotion, such as a smiley face for happiness or a frowning face for sadness. Repeat the word and the definition several times while the two students continue to act it out. Continue in a like manner with three additional words.

Do four words per day for three consecutive days. On the fourth day, have students study in groups of three or four. Give them index cards and have them create three columns on the cards labeled Word, Face, and Definition. One group member chooses a word and acts it out, and the rest of the group writes the definition and draws a representation of it on their cards (see Figure 12). Students rotate until all 12 words have been covered—at least two words acted per student.

On the day of the exam, give students 5 to 10 minutes to review the words one more time. In most cases, this routine will result in impressive pass rates for even the most struggling students.

Enrichment

The fundamental structure underlying Face Reading—high repetition, linguistic definition, group thinking, and graphic representation—can be readily adapted for words other than adjectives. For example, I have also used the same kind of procedures (replacing facial expressions with group pantomime) to teach commonly used Latin words and phrases, such as *ad infinitum, tabula rasa, dulce bellum inexpertis,* and *aut disce aut discede.*

ADJECTIVES FOR FACIAL EXPRESSIONS

1. amiable

2. circumspect

3. diffident

4. disconsolate

5. dolorous

6. dowdy

7. euphoric

8. exultant

9. intrepid

10. jocular

11. jubilant

12. lachrymose

13. lackadaisical

14. languid

15. loquacious

16. mirthful

17. morose

18. perplexed

19. phlegmatic

20. solemn

21. staid

22. timorous

23. wrathful

24. wretched

Dances With Words

Type of Activity
Group

Approximate Time
One 50-minute class period

Objective
Students will learn a litany of precise, useful action words.

Summary
It is difficult to fall asleep while dancing. This fact alone gives Dances With Words great allure for teachers of adolescents. By connecting physical actions to words, Dances With Words exemplifies the power of action verbs, eases the abstract nature of language, and gives a sense of urgency to matching movement to word. It is also a great deal of fun.

Materials
Find two songs online or on CDs you have at home or can borrow from the library that are associated with specific dance steps. Songs like "Chicken Dance" or "Cupid Shuffle" work well, especially when paired with ballroom dances, such as the foxtrot, waltz, and tango. Other song suggestions are "The Blue Danube" (or another waltz by Johann Strauss), "La Cumparsita" (tango), and "New York, New York" (foxtrot). The exercise works best if the songs provide great contrast.

You'll also need copies of the Dance Verbs handout (see p. 106).

Setup
Have copies of the Dance Verbs handout on hand and two songs ready to play.

Procedure

Teach students the specific dance steps to a song. I recommend beginning with a contemporary song, if possible. Go through the dance routine at least four times, until students are able to do it independently.

Divide students into groups of three or four. Student roles include the watcher (polices duplication, rejects nonverbs), the writer (neatly writes down the verbs called out by members of the group), the speaker (reports the results to class), and the wordsmith leader (provides the words; actually all students contribute words, but this is a useful role if you use four students per group).

Tell students that after they dance, they are to list as many action verbs as they can that relate to the movement of the dance and the dancers in their group. Let them know that only root words count; tense variations, such as *ran*, *running*, and *have run*, count as duplication and are not allowed. As a kind of last-minute help, give each student the Dance Verbs handout and explain the meanings of each term. Include at least 10 SAT-type vocabulary words on the list.

After the dance, give students 5 minutes to complete their writing and format their lists of verbs in a readable format. Then, have each group sum the number of distinct words in their group. Each group states the number of words they wrote and reads their final list aloud. Groups lose 1 point for every duplicated word. Be generous with regard to nonverbs. Verbing (trying to turn a noun into a verb) can be fun and enlightening. For example, many words in English, such as *slouch*, *party*, and *goof*, can serve as either nouns or verbs.

Particularly praise descriptive words. Tell students that you are going to do the process one more time, this time with a different song. Teach students another dance step that's radically different from the first one. Follow the same procedure as with the first song: rehearsal, dance, write action verbs for 5 minutes, sum the number of words, read the lists aloud, emphasize particularly descriptive words.

With Dances With Words, the denouement is key. Ask students to note the variety of action words recorded in both dances and emphasize the expressive power of action words compared with forms of *to be* and passive verbs. Also, compare the actions implicit in the verbs of the two lists. While many words will be the same, there should be some obvious differences based on the contrasts in the music, tempo, and dance routines.

Enrichment

Dances With Words is a particularly good fit for English-language learners. Vary the Dance Verbs list according to students' competency level in English. For example, consider having students describe the music using the Adjectives for Dance Music handout (see p. 107). Students should select at least seven adjectives that describe the music and defend their choices by explaining their feelings about the music. Of course, students take special pride in slamming songs like "Chicken Dance."

DANCE VERBS

1. bob

2. bound

3. caper

4. cavort

5. convulse

6. dodder

7. frolic

8. gambol

9. gyrate

10. jaunt

11. joggle

12. jounce

13. prance

14. promenade

15. pulsate

16. quaver

17. quiver

18. revel

19. romp

20. saunter

21. stall

22. stroll

23. strut

24. traipse

25. undulate

26. whirl

ADJECTIVES FOR DANCE MUSIC

1. alluring

2. anguished

3. antiquated

4. appalling

5. archaic

6. beguiling

7. cacophonous

8. clamorous

9. discordant

10. dulcet

11. elegant

12. engrossing

13. euphonious

14. exquisite

15. grating

16. grotesque

17. harmonious

18. inane

19. laudable

20. mellifluous

21. mesmerizing

22. overwrought

23. pedestrian

24. shrill

25. soporific

26. torpid

Soul and Sense Poetry

Type of Activity
Individual and group

Approximate Time
One 50-minute class period

Objective
Students will use words that appeal to the five senses to describe themselves and others, their dispositions, and their values and will learn to improve the precision of their descriptions.

Summary
In addition to allowing students to discover how others feel about them, Soul and Sense Poetry gets students to think in novel ways about words and the myriad levels on which words can communicate. This activity is useful for classes of students who have yet to venture much beyond long lists of adjectives in their descriptive writing.

Materials
Pen and paper

Setup
Have students write a list of words that describe both their inner and outer selves. This usually takes about 10 minutes.

Ask students if they believe that humans have souls. What does a soul look like? What does it sound like? (If some students seem uncomfortable with the term *soul*, allow them to substitute *attitude* or *outlook on life*.) Next, tell students that they are going to describe their souls, attitudes, or outlooks on life by describing themselves (their appearance, accomplishments, likes, and dislikes) through the five senses: smell, taste, touch, sight, and hearing.

Write a set of descriptive words on the board about yourself as an example, such as *happy, sloppy, skinny, athletic, tennis player, brother,* and *likes tie-dyed T-shirts.* Identify that *happy, sloppy, skinny,* and *athletic* are adjectives, *tennis player* and *brother* are nouns, and *likes tie-dyed T-shirts* is a phrase. Tell students that all the parts of speech are acceptable in creating their initial lists.

Next, ask students which of the words on the board specifically appeal to one of the five senses. Most students will acknowledge that most of the words seem to appeal to a sense of sight or to no sense at all. Write the following on the board:

happy = smell =

sloppy = taste =

skinny = touch =

athletic = sight =

tennis player = sound =

Tell students to give a concrete example of how each word could be described through a particular sense. For example, a happy smell might be freshly buttered popcorn or cotton candy. A sloppy taste might be eating a huge taco with one hand while trying to drive a car down a busy freeway with the other.

Have students "sensitize" their self-descriptions by attempting to connect words with one of the five senses, as mentioned earlier. For this part of the activity, allow students to join up with others in groups of three or four. If possible, allow them to choose their own groups, but no group should contain more than four members.

Procedure

Students should not show their lists to others in their group.

One member of the group is the focus of every group member's writing for 5 to 8 minutes. Students should attempt to describe aspects of the person with which they are familiar by first generating lists of words, then going back and sensitizing their lists. While other members of the group write lists of words that describe the student in focus, the focus student takes out the original self-made list and adds to it. After time has

Figure 13. Two Seventh-Grade Students' Soul and Sense Poems

My soul is ghostly white
looks like a fog at night
sounds like the whistling wind
coming 'round the darkly-lit bend.
Smells like tomato plants
but tastes like chocolate covered ants
feels like evaporating dew
nobody knew
what it has been through.

My soul would smell like fresh air
never stink, God, I swear
would feel like a cloud
soft, but not a shroud
a snow white pillow soft as cotton
when it feels good, it's rotten.

elapsed, have each member of the group give their list to the person who was the focus for writing. The focus rotates until each student has lists from all members of the group.

Each student may draw from any of these lists as he or she writes a poem that describes his or her soul, attitude, or outlook on life. The poem may be rhyming or nonrhyming. Figure 13 shows two strong student examples of these types of poems.

Enrichment

A wonderful exercise is to allow students to make short videos of their soul and sense poetry. Through video, students can mix images, music, words, and sounds to construct a unique, highly personal statement.

Vocab War

Type of Activity
Group

Approximate Time
One 50-minute class period

Objective
Students will increase vocabulary, learn cognitive reasoning skills, uncover analogous relationships, become proficient in all uses of the dictionary, learn to use synonyms and antonyms, and increase spelling and pronunciation skills.

Summary
When first developed, Vocab War was intended to be used primarily as an occasional break from the traditional vocabulary approach of having students look up a list of words, write definitions, and then use the words in context sentences. What quickly became apparent after playing this game weekly for several weeks was that not only were students remembering the key vocabulary words and using them in class, but also they looked forward to playing and were becoming experts at using dictionaries.

With each week, the game became more successful, as did the need to establish some clearly defined rules of play. Listed with this activity are the rules and rewards I have developed during the four years I have been using it. These rules are only suggested, but have proven to be successful in maximizing the learning potential for this game.

Although this game may have started out as a means of broadening my approach to teaching vocabulary, it has evolved into a weekly event that many of my students look forward to. I now keep a scoreboard in my classroom and have my classes battle one another for high score of the week. For added incentive, on the Monday after a game, I test my students on the previous week's five keywords using a multiple-choice combination of definitions and synonyms from the game, and I exempt my winning class from that test. This has been so successful as a motivator that I now exempt from the test the group with the high score in each of my classes.

Fridays have become Vocab War Day in my classes, and it is completely normal for students to stop in throughout the day to get a jump on the keywords so that they may come to class ready to begin matching the synonyms and antonyms. In some cases, students have even been known to leave a false list of the matched words in their dictionaries, hoping to fool a student coming into the next class period. As a result of this game, many of my students have begun using many of the vocabulary words from the game in their daily conversations. Students also quickly begin showing a willingness and comfort toward using a dictionary for the simplest of assignments without being told or asked to use one.

Materials

A dictionary of synonyms and antonyms (from your library or bookstore) and a set of dictionaries

Setup

Use the dictionary of synonyms and antonyms to select five words that are appropriate for the class. Select three synonyms and three antonyms to go with each of these five words. For example, in the game that follows, the word *zeal* was selected. With this word are the synonyms *fervor*, *haste*, and *spirit*, and antonyms *lethargy*, *apathy*, and *torpor*. The original five words selected will become the keywords to the game (these are usually the words I hold the students responsible to learn), and the synonyms and antonyms will be the words the students must match to these keywords.

On one side of the chalkboard, write the five keywords across the top and create a chart similar to the one presented in Figure 14, which includes five keywords that I have used with my regular ninth-grade English class.

On the other side of the chalkboard, list the synonyms and antonyms that match the five keywords in a random order similar to the following

Figure 14. Example of a Keyword Chart

respite		graphic		enervate	
Synonyms	Antonyms	Synonyms	Antonyms	Synonyms	Antonyms
interlude pause cessation	gradation course progression	picturesque vivid explicit	obscure dubious enigmatic	paralyze attenuate debilitate	inspirit animate incite

mental		slander	
Synonyms	Antonyms	Synonyms	Antonyms
percipient intellectual rational	incogitant fatuous inane	asperse vilify belittle	eulogize exalt advocate

columns. Feel free to substitute "S" and "A" for "Synonyms" and "Antonyms," respectively, when writing on the board.

advocate	vivid	cessation	debilitate
fatuous	paralyze	inspirit	rational
attenuate	picturesque	obscure	eulogize
interlude	incogitant	belittle	incite
dubious	course	intellectual	progression
percipient	animate	vilify	inane
asperse	enigmatic	exalt	explicit
pause	gradation		

Procedure

Part 1

Instruct students to use their dictionaries to look up the definitions for the five keywords. Once the students have successfully looked up a keyword, they should write the definition in words they will understand; this first part is essential to the success of each group and the game. Having done this, each group should divide the columns of synonyms and antonyms, and each group member is responsible for looking up the words in his or her designated column.

At this point, explain to the groups the process of matching the synonyms and antonyms to the keywords. (It is normal for there to be some confusion with the introduction of this activity, but most students will catch on quickly, especially once the game gets going.) As simply as possible, explain that each group member should begin looking up his or her column one word at a time. Once they find the first word in their column, students should consult their written definition of the first keyword. It is not necessary for the group members to write any definitions for their respective column words, but they should compare the dictionary definitions against their written definitions of their keywords. The idea is to look at the two words and reason whether they have similar meanings.

If the two words clearly have similar meanings, each student should list his or her column word as a synonym for the keyword it matches. But if the meanings aren't similar, he or she should then consider if the column word's meaning is the opposite of their keyword. If it's clear that the column word belongs under the keyword as an antonym, then it gets listed in the antonym column. If the first word of his or her column does not fit as a synonym *or* antonym of the first keyword, then the student should move on to the second keyword and repeat the process. Instruct students to repeat these steps until all words in their columns have been identified and matched to their proper keywords.

Part 2

After all groups have been given half the class period to look up and match synonyms and antonyms, it is time to begin the game. Tell students to continue looking up words when the game begins, but at this point, they also should begin to focus as a group on what words they have matched, what words are being put on the chalkboard by other groups, and what words they still need to match. The game then proceeds as follows.

Select a group to begin. One member of the selected group will then have 60 seconds to go to the chalkboard and write a synonym or antonym in its appropriate column. The groups are not informed if they are correct or not; they simply put a word on the board then take their seats. Scoring will occur during the course of the game, so don't tell the kids now if their words are correct or not. If the word placed on the board is correct, the group will receive 1 point, but if it is incorrect, the group will receive no points. Once the first group is finished, it is the second group's turn.

The second group, like the first group, also will have 60 seconds to place a synonym or antonym in its appropriate column, only they first have the option of erasing the first word from the board if they feel it is in the wrong column. To do this, they must first pronounce the word correctly and ask permission to erase it. If the word is pronounced incorrectly, whether it is in the right column or not, inform the group member that he or she has pronounced it wrong and ask him or her to take a seat; the group's turn is forfeited, and the class still does not know if the word is in the correct column. If the word is pronounced correctly but is in the correct column, inform the group member that the word is correct where it is, he or she must take a seat, and the group's turn is forfeited. If the word is pronounced correctly and is in the wrong column, the group member may erase it and then place any word he or she wishes under any column. The student does not have to replace or place the word she has erased. If a group is not certain and does not wish to risk it, the students are not required to identify a misplaced word, but instead may simply use their turn to place a synonym or antonym in the column in which they feel it belongs.

If a group correctly identifies a misplaced word and correctly places a word under its correct keyword, the group receives 2 points instead of 1. If a group correctly identifies a misplaced word but misplaces the synonym or antonym it chooses to write on the board, the group receives 0 points.

Once the second group has finished its turn at the board, the third group has 60 seconds to take its turn, following the procedures above. The game proceeds until all the synonyms and antonyms have been correctly placed under their keywords, or until time runs out. A competitive class will occasionally finish the game with about 5 minutes to spare during a 50-minute period, which is the same amount of time you should leave for scoring and summary.

To help the game, ask a group to circle a column once it contains the three proper synonyms or antonyms. No points are given for circling a column; it is merely a courtesy to the players to help them identify and concentrate on the remaining words. This will also allow the more competitive groups to focus on identifying a misplaced word under a column that has three words in it and is not circled.

Rules of the Game

- Each group has 60 seconds to take its turn.
- Any word placed on the board that is already in a circled column will result in the loss of 1 point.
- Misspelled words are considered incorrect.
- Anyone wishing to erase a word from the board must first ask permission and pronounce the word correctly (including misspelled words).
- No group member may talk to anyone outside of his or her group during the entire course of the game; to do so results in the loss of 1 point.
- Group members may correct and talk to their representative member while he or she is at the chalkboard.
- Only one member from each group may go the chalkboard during the group's turn, and each group must rotate who goes up each turn.
- If a group does not have a word to place on the board when it is their turn, they may attempt to erase an incorrect word without having to place a word on the board. No points may be scored for doing this, and the chance for a perfect game is forfeit, but no points are lost for passing.

Points and Scoring

- Students earn 1 point for a word identified and placed under the correct keyword.
- Students earn 2 points for correctly identifying, pronouncing, and erasing a word, then placing a word correctly on the board. If a group successfully erases a word but misses the word they place on the board, no points are given.
- A group will lose 1 point if any member talks to anyone outside of the group during the game.

- A group will lose 1 point if it places a word on the board that has already been placed in a column that is circled.
- A group will lose 1 point if it passes on its turn.
- If a group plays a perfect game, makes no mistakes, and loses no points, its score is doubled.

Thinking Sentences

Type of Activity
Group

Approximate Time
One 50-minute class period

Objective
Students will increase vocabulary, use difficult words in context, develop reasoning skills, and demonstrate how to write and use complex sentences.

Summary
This activity has produced some remarkable short stories. Most students enjoy Thinking Sentences, and there is usually a high level of collaboration within each group. It is not uncommon for the students to ask if they can read their stories aloud, and I usually have a person from each group read the stories aloud after everyone has finished.

   Having the students read their stories aloud is also a clever means to sneak in a lesson on pronunciation and how to use the dictionary.

Materials
Pen and paper, and a set of dictionaries

Setup
Write a creative prompt on the chalkboard that will help stimulate the writing of a short story, for example:

   Everything was perfect until the first one fell from the sky.

   Next, list several nouns and adjectives on the chalkboard. It is up to you to select words that are suitably challenging for your students. It is also helpful to include the part of speech for each word. The following list is a sample of words I have used with my average ninth graders:

esoteric (adj.)	placebo (n.)	subtle (adj.)
existential (adj.)	illusion (n.)	eloquent (adj.)
substratum (n.)	ironic (adj.)	luminary (n.)
phylum (n.)	obstinate (adj.)	atrocity (n.)

Procedure

Students select a member from their group to begin their short stories. This student is to copy the story prompt from the board, and then follow that prompt with the next two sentences of the story, which come from the student's own imagination. The student must use one of the words from the chalkboard in one of his or her two sentences and use it correctly in context.

Once the student has written two sentences using one of the vocabulary words in one of them, he or she should pass the story to the left within the group, and the student receiving the story must add two more sentences to the story. He or she, too, must use one of the vocabulary words within one of these two new sentences. Students should not select a word that has already been used, and advise students not to add suffixes or prefixes to any of the words, as that may change the part of speech, and the focus of this lesson's objectives would then begin to blur.

Continue the activity until either time runs out or all words from the chalkboard have been used. Inform students that when the story comes around to them, it is their job to check their peers' grammar. If a mistake is found, the reader should return the paper to the person who made the mistake and politely point it out so that it may be fixed.

Enrichment

An idea that has worked well in conjunction with Thinking Sentences is to require students to begin one of their sentences with a subordinating conjunction, which forces them to write a complex sentence, and to use one of the vocabulary words in a second sentence. For example, I might write this on the board:

As I made my way through the airport crowd to gate 32, I bumped into a wild-eyed, old woman wearing a bright purple sweater.

Next, I might solicit another example from students and write that on the board as well.

Visuals:
Connecting Writing and Art

We live in a blitz of mediated images. Pictures fill our newspapers, magazines, books, clothing, billboards, TV screens, and computer monitors as never before in the history of mass communications. We are becoming a visually mediated society. For many, understanding of the world is being accomplished, not by reading words, but by reading images.

From *Visual Communication: Images With Messages* by Paul Lester

You are not afraid of using technology, exactly. It may be true that you've never been sure how to use the remote controls for your stereo, DVD player, and television at home, but you could learn how if you thought there might be a payoff. You can make them work when you need to. No need to go overboard and actually read the instructions.

You like film, you have a page on Facebook, and you've noticed that screens now suddenly seem to dominate the cultural landscape: computers, cellular phones, tiny iPod screens, massive electronic billboards, and gigantic, life-size, high-definition televisions. There are screens in restaurants, hospitals, airports, groceries, clothing stores, electronics stores, schools, and even libraries. You're not sure whether you should offer your classroom as a sanctuary against screens or as a research center for their analysis and evaluation.

Being a bohemian, you cannot deny the power of the image and the influence of screens on your students' perceptions of truth and reality. A word is a word, but an image is irrefutable.

The planet is evolving. To keep the written word alive—to keep literature, language, and composition relevant—you must reformulate some of your lessons, so they engage students through the visual, and then take them to vistas you want them to know: the undiscovered country of words, contemplation, and ideas.

Once you begin the trek, there is no turning back. Your students will respond enthusiastically when you ask them to paint or react to a painting, when you ask them to translate images into words, when you ask them to consider how an image affects thought and emotion. You love images, but you are an English teacher not a cinematographer. The image is not the goal; the image is the vehicle.

Adagio in Your Back Pocket

Type of Activity
Individual

Approximate Time
One 50-minute class period

Objective
Students will attach images and words to music.

Summary
Samuel Barber's "Adagio for Strings" is perhaps the saddest piece of classical music ever written and has been used in the films *Platoon*, *Sicko*, and *The Scarlet Letter*, as well as television shows such as *Seinfeld*, *ER*, *South Park*, and three episodes of *The Simpsons*. Through music, image, and word, Adagio in Your Back Pocket often enables reluctant writers to create a solid base of ideas for subsequent writing.

Materials
Drawing paper, pens, crayons, and a recording of Barber's "Adagio for Strings" (I recommend Leonard Bernstein and the New York Philharmonic's version.)

Setup
Tell students that you are going to play a piece of music and that you want them to think about what story the music is trying to convey. Does the music evoke sadness, joy, or another emotion?

Procedure
Give every student a blank, 8½" × 11" sheet of paper. Students fold the paper in half. They are to draw on the left side and write on the right side.

Play "Adagio for Strings." Ask students to create an abstract drawing. The drawing need not be artistically brilliant or realistic, but should accurately reflect the feeling and tone of the music. Especially encourage the use of colors. After the music ends, give students 5 minutes to finish their drawings.

Play the song a second time. Ask students to describe in words at least seven images and the colors suggested by the music on the right side of the paper.

Have students show their art and read their descriptions of images to the class. It usually works best if students explain their drawings first, then read what they wrote. Repeat or write on the board any particularly effective phrases or astute descriptions. After several students have shared

Figure 15. A Ninth-Grade Student's Work for the Adagio in Your Back Pocket Activity

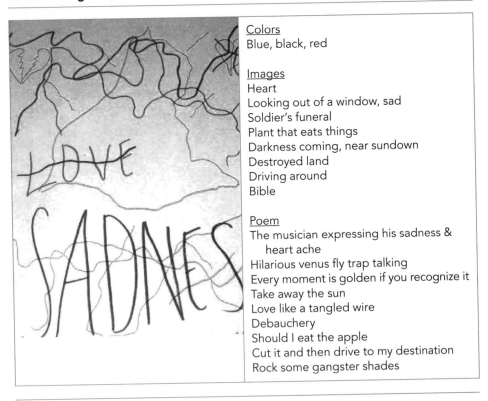

Colors
Blue, black, red

Images
Heart
Looking out of a window, sad
Soldier's funeral
Plant that eats things
Darkness coming, near sundown
Destroyed land
Driving around
Bible

Poem
The musician expressing his sadness & heart ache
Hilarious venus fly trap talking
Every moment is golden if you recognize it
Take away the sun
Love like a tangled wire
Debauchery
Should I eat the apple
Cut it and then drive to my destination
Rock some gangster shades

their work, summarize and synthesize students' comments about "Adagio for Strings." You may want to ask what recent story or poem you've read in class for which the music would serve as an appropriate soundtrack.

Students enjoy this activity and tend to take ownership of both their drawings and poems. Thus, you will inevitably see students fold up their papers and put them in their back pockets. A ninth-grade student drew and wrote the work shown in Figure 15.

Enrichment

Once students have established their palettes of images and words, they can easily transfer them into poetry or narrative. I am fond of poetic forms, such as the pantoum, for such assignments, although it is easiest just to have students transfer their images into words and workshop each line (removing clichés and adding precise language) into a free verse poem. The ninth-grade student's poem in Figure 15 is a free verse poem, which was completed in a single, 50-minute class (including the time spent listening to "Adagio for Strings" twice).

Solitude of the Soul

Type of Activity
Individual

Approximate Time
One 50-minute class period

Objective
Students will think about a topic that has fascinated writers, religious leaders, and mystics for eternity—the constitution of the soul.

Summary
Many teachers may prefer to have students fill in an adjectives worksheet rather than ponder the nature of the soul. After all, the concept of soul might be construed as a controversial topic, although most of us would agree that a person's soul is more important than an adjectives worksheet.

Elizabeth Cady Stanton's work, including the speech to Congress excerpted here, led to the establishment of the 19th Amendment to the United States Constitution, which gave women the right to vote in 1920. If she had circled adjectives instead of pondering her soul, the United States may have been slower to end its discrimination against women.

Materials
A photo or replica of Lorado Taft's sculpture *The Solitude of the Soul*, copies of the Excerpts of Solitude handout (see p. 129), and a poem or song lyrics that you can choose or let the students choose as homework

The full versions of the Stanton speech and Shakur poem, as well as an image of Taft's sculpture, can be retrieved from the websites listed under Resources at the end of this lesson.

Setup

Have your or the students' chosen poem or song lyrics, a photo or replica of the sculpture *The Solitude of the Soul*, and the Excerpts of Solitude handout ready.

Procedure

If you choose to let the students select a poem or song lyrics, briefly explain this activity the day before, so they can come to class with their chosen piece in hand.

Read aloud the excerpt from Shakur's (1999) "In the Depths of Solitude (Dedicated 2 Me)." Discuss the themes and images. (*Note:* If you go on Google Books and search for the book noted in the Resources section, you'll see a typeset version of this poem in the book preview, along with a handwritten version by Shakur that the kids might be interested in seeing because he drew visuals for a few of the words.)

Discuss with students Taft's (1914) sculpture *The Solitude of the Soul*. Ask students what the sculpture expresses. Have students compare the poem by Shakur with the physical aspects of the sculpture.

Next, students read the excerpt from Stanton's (1892) speech to Congress, in which she describes the private, powerful, impenetrable "inner being" possessed by all humans.

Students take a favorite line from each piece—the poem by Shakur, the speech by Stanton, and the additional poem or song—and translate them into their own words. Then, students add a fourth line that expresses their own vision of the soul.

Have students use this four-line poem as an introduction to an essay in which they attempt to answer, What is the nature of the soul? To answer that question, students should also consider, How is a person's soul different from his or her personality? or How is a person's soul different from his or her brain? Figure 16 demonstrates an 11th grader's work.

Enrichment

This assignment leads nicely into poetry writing or essay writing on the "nature of the soul." Essays by transcendentalists, such as Ralph Waldo Emerson, Henry David Thoreau, and Margaret Fuller, and stoics, such as Marcus Aurelius and Epictetus, would add interesting perspectives.

Figure 16. An 11th Grader's Solitude of the Soul Poem and Essay

The premise for the student's poem:

Line 1 (chosen from Shakur's poem): a young heart with an old soul
Line 2 (chosen from Stanton's speech): Our inner being, which we call ourself, no eye nor touch of man or angel has ever pierced.
Line 3 (chosen from an additional poem): Seeking through art what life cannot bestow—
Line 4 (written by the student as his vision of the soul): The soul dies when the body dies.

The lines above translated poetically by the student and the student's essay:

The lines are not on my face, but scar my soul
True self is a stranger
Creating dreams in stories
All is dust, all returns to dust.

It is like always reaching for something, but never being able to touch it. The figures in the sculpture, the lines from Tupac, Stanton, and the third poem on the soul. They act like the soul is a wandering ghost, but it is not. The soul is substantial—it is basically who you are beyond looks, money, and status. You may not be able to touch it or take a photo of it, but it is there.

Sometimes I feel like friendships are built on a meeting of the souls—I do not know any other way to explain why I have the friends I do. We do not like the same things or the same people. We do not look alike. We do not have the same values or beliefs. But, sometimes when I look into a friend's eyes, there is a kind of connection. I think it is a meeting of souls.

You can remember details for a history test, and you can memorize complicated formulas for math, but these do not involve the soul—they involve the brain. When you look into someone's eyes, it is the soul you see, not the brain.

Sometimes my brain tells me to do one thing, but my soul tells me to do another. For example, when I see the homeless guy asking for change at the intersection, my brain tells me that if I give the guy a dollar, he will go buy beer or drugs or something. But, my soul says, "Hey the guy needs some help. Let's give him a buck."

RESOURCES

Shakur, T. (1999). "In the depths of solitude (dedicated 2 me)." In *The rose that grew from concrete* (pp. 4–5). New York: Pocket. Retrieved April 13, 2010, from books .simonandschuster.com/Rose-That-Grew-From-Concrete/Tupac-Shakur/ 9780671028442/excerpt/1

Stanton, E.C. (1892, January 18). *Solitude of self.* Address to the U.S. Congressional Judicial Committee. Retrieved February 15, 2010, from www.pbs.org/stanton anthony/resources/index.html?body=solitude_self.html

Taft, L. (1914). *The solitude of the soul* [Sculpture]. Retrieved February 15, 2010, from www.artic.edu/aic/collections/artwork/70466

EXCERPTS OF SOLITUDE

Excerpt from "In the Depths of Solitude (Dedicated 2 Me)" by Tupac Shakur:

I exist in the depths of solitude
pondering my true goal
Trying 2 find peace of mind
and still preserve my soul
CONSTANTLY yearning 2 be accepted
and from all receive respect
Never compromising but sometimes risky
and that is my only regret

Excerpted from "In the Depths of Solitude (Dedicated 2 Me)," by T. Shakur, 1999, on *The Rose That Grew From Concrete* (pp. 4–5), New York: Pocket.

Excerpt from "Solitude of Self" by Elizabeth Cady Stanton:

I remember once, in crossing the Atlantic, to have gone upon the deck of the ship at midnight, when a dense black cloud enveloped the sky, and the great deep was roaring madly under the lashes of demoniac winds. My feeling was not of danger or fear (which is a base surrender of the immortal soul), but of utter desolation and loneliness; a little speck of life shut in by a tremendous darkness. Again I remember to have climbed the slopes of the Swiss Alps, up beyond the point where vegetation ceases, and the stunted conifers no longer struggle against the unfeeling blasts. Around me lay a huge confusion of rocks, out of which the gigantic ice peaks shot into the measureless blue of the heavens, and again my only feeling was the awful solitude.

And yet, there is a solitude, which each and every one of us has always carried with him, more inaccessible than the ice-cold mountains, more profound than the midnight sea; the solitude of self. Our inner being, which we call ourself, no eye nor touch of man or angel has ever pierced. It is more hidden than the caves of the gnome; the sacred adytum of the oracle; the hidden chamber of eleusinian mystery, for to it only omniscience is permitted to enter. Such is individual life. Who, I ask you, can take, dare take, on himself the rights, the duties, the responsibilities of another human soul?

Excerpted from "Solitude of Self," by E.C. Stanton, January 18, 1892, address to the U.S. Congressional Judiciary Committee, retrieved February 9, 2010, from www.pbs.org/stantonanthony/resources/index.html?body=solitude_self.html.

Monster Mayhem:
Scary Stories for October

Type of Activity
Individual

Approximate Time
Four 50-minute class periods

Objective
Students will create and analyze characters within fiction, create settings for plot and conflict, and write critically with appropriate tone and effective description.

Summary
Monster Mayhem is something I've done for 15 years now, and I still get excited every year when it's time to introduce the assignment. When the kids write, I play some Halloween sound effects and selected music from scary movies. It's all a bit cheesy at first, but the students end up loving the assignment. I've turned it into a contest in which each peer review group selects one story for reading, and the kids vote on the finalists. The final winners are decided by the supreme authority in my household: my lovely wife, who has enjoyed being a part of the assignment for as long as I've done it.

The students will need a minute to absorb the assignment, but will also be extremely excited. This is a type of writing they don't get to do that often. It requires a good deal of critical thinking and imagination, but also helps them understand the importance of character and setting within the plot of a story. I emphasize the rule that no one dies in their stories. I let them work that out, which eliminates the ease of simply killing characters to move the story along. I also encourage the students not to create more than two main characters so that they don't make more work for themselves, or confuse the story, more than is needed.

Finally, I make the urban legend part of the assignment optional to reach a B or an A on the assignment. This will give those students who are likely to struggle with the writing a break and help them focus on creating a story line that is very doable. Typically, the final stories will average seven to eight pages, although I avoid giving length requirements. I do provide a sample from the previous year's contest winner, and these are usually well over 10 pages. I begin the assignment two weeks before Halloween and plan it so that I can announce a winner on or before Halloween.

Materials

Pen and paper, or a computer with word-processing software, crayons (if available), and copies of the Monster Mayhem handout (see p. 133)

Setup

Students will need a basic understanding of urban legends to complete this assignment. I recommend that you spend a half hour discussing and defining urban legends, and showing examples, which are readily available on the Internet.

Procedure

It should be noted that the first step of this lesson is based on an activity in *In the Middle* by Nancie Atwell (1998).

First, instruct students to take out a piece of paper and write a one-page description of the scariest monster they can imagine. For this activity, tell students not to put their names on their paper and to make sure they write every detail, color, smell, or whatever that will help the reader see the monster they are describing. Give the class approximately a half hour to complete this, then collect all of the descriptions. Next, hand out blank sheets of paper (and provide crayons if you have them), along with the monster descriptions in random order. Instruct the students to read the descriptions and to each do their best to draw a picture of the monster they are reading about.

Once all students have drawn pictures, have them put their names on the drawings and staple them to the monster descriptions. Then, hold up the pictures one by one and ask the students to identify their monsters. Typically, the students do this fairly easy, and I enjoy letting the kids see the variety of monsters that have been created.

When all students have their own monsters back in hand, begin the character assignments for their monster stories. First, have the students select two numbers between 1 and 7, and tell them to write these on the top of a piece of paper, one on top of the other. These will be the two characters they are to use within a story. Next, have the students select one letter between A and D, and write that letter below the previous two. This will be the setting where most of their stories are to take place.

When all students have selected their numbers and letters, read the characters aloud, telling students to write the names of their characters next to their numbers; they'll get the details in a handout. After the characters are read, announce the settings.

At this point, give all students the Monster Mayhem handout and go over the rules. They are to write a scary story that uses their monsters, their two characters, and one setting (based on the handout), and bring the characters to the settings where they actually meet the monsters and engage in the ensuing mayhem. As an option for a B or A grade on the monster story, tell the students that they can create an urban legend about their monsters and settings, which must be incorporated into their story,

Enrichment

I recommend building a relevant focus into the assignment. For example, we usually study Edgar Allen Poe in my sophomore class at the time of this assignment. Within the rules, I add the following:

   6. All stories *must* creatively incorporate several lines or a passage from an Edgar Allen Poe poem as some type of clue or symbol important to the story.

This adds some relevance to the work we've been doing and also requires the students to research, and think about, poetry by Poe.

RESOURCE
Atwell, N. (1998). *In the middle: New understandings about writing, reading, and learning* (2nd ed.). Portsmouth, NH: Boynton/Cook.

MONSTER MAYHEM

Characters:

1. Disco Dean is a 64-year-old security guard who breaks out singing disco oldies at the top of his lungs. He also dances very enthusiastically while singing.

2. China is an 81-year-old Cajun voodoo priestess.

3. Vlad is a 22-year-old video store clerk who is an avid member of a Goth wanna-be vampire club. He's also a chronic narcoleptic.

4. Ophelia is a 33-year-old librarian who randomly and compulsively kisses her fingers and whispers to her hands.

5. Morgul is a 51-year-old man who believes (and dresses like) he is Death. He constantly walks the streets, touching people as he walks past them, hoping they will die.

6. Cat is a 24-year-old fashion model who believes that she turns into a cat at night. After dark, she meows loudly and constantly, purrs randomly, and claws people without warning.

7. Dr. Lycan is a 31-year-old zoologist who believes he is a werewolf. When the moon is full, he impulsively runs about howling like a wolf and biting people at random.

Settings:

A. Nighttime with a full moon at an old, abandoned church in the woods

B. Nighttime with a full moon at an old, forgotten summer camp with a small, overgrown lake, deep in the woods

C. Nighttime with a full moon at an old, forgotten cemetery in the woods

D. Nighttime with a full moon at a hidden cave on the California coast

Rules:

• Stories must include your monster creation, your two characters, and your setting!

• Those wishing for a B or A grade must create and incorporate an urban legend based on their assigned setting and their monster.

• All stories must attempt to be descriptive and entertaining.

• No killing is allowed in the story. (You can creatively lead the readers to make their own conclusions without actually writing the act.)

• Gross-out writing is acceptable for this assignment. (Leading readers to make their own conclusions is often more effective in being gross.)

From *Going Bohemian: How to Teach Writing Like You Mean It* (2nd edition) by Lawrence Baines & Anthony Kunkel. Copyright 2010 International Reading Association.

Photo Essay

Type of Activity
Individual

Approximate Time
One or two 50-minute class periods

Plan for one day of demonstration and another day in which you help students put projects together. Otherwise, you can use this as a project on which students work when they have a little extra time at the end of class. I recommend assigning the project one week ahead of the due date to allow students who "really get into it" to produce the kind of photo essay that they envision.

Objective
Students will learn to write effective expository text and extend through words what is obvious through image.

Summary
Photo essays are a fun, effective way to get students to think and write informatively. Perhaps no other activity in this book addresses so directly the relationship of word to image. Thus, Photo Essay is an ideal activity for both English-language learners and struggling readers. Photo essays are also superb artifacts for open house, especially if they pertain to the community or school.

Projects can range from a photojournalistic investigation into a local problem, such as homelessness, to an instructional manual on how to care for a dog. A student of mine who whined whenever he had to write more than a sentence in class once created a detailed "secret guide" to the video game *World of Warcraft* in excess of 100 pages.

Materials
Students must have access to a digital camera or a device that takes photos (cell phone, music player, or similar devices work well). I urge you to give approval to topics *before* cameras are handed out.

You'll also need copies of the Photo Essay Evaluation handout (see p. 139).

Setup

Students enjoy viewing completed photo essays. Displaying an exemplary photo essay on a bulletin board or in a slide show can give students an idea of expectations for their finished products.

Procedure

Send a letter to parents notifying them of your intent to have your students do a photo essay that will likely involve a device capable of taking photos.

In class, announce that the photo essay assignment will be due in one week. Ask students what is meant by the adage "a picture is worth a thousand words."

Discuss the roles of words and pictures. Show students some how-to books that use photographs and text. Many home repair books use a text and photo format, as do how-to sports books, especially tennis and golf.

Show students excerpts from the example essay, "How to Solve a Rubik's Cube," in Figure 17, which a ninth-grade student created using 29 photos with textual explanations (only 10 are shown in the figure). Point out to the students that the original was in color, not black and white as shown here.

Ask students to write out five possible subjects for their photo essays. Potential subjects for essays should be accessible and available for photographs. Approve or disapprove the students' topics.

Although students will claim that they already know how to shoot a photo, show them some fundamentals with regard to cameras, such as focus, lighting, speed, and especially distance from the subject. Students should be encouraged to shoot close-ups, although they will initially tend to shoot everything from a distance.

Before students begin work on their projects, ask to see their photographs. Do not accept poor photographs. After students have their approved photos, demonstrate how to write text that would accompany a photo essay, including some emphasis on page design. Writing should not only explain the photograph but also extend the meaning.

Rest assured, you will have to give extensions to some students for terrible photos or for not having done the assignment at all. However, once

Figure 17. Excerpts From a Ninth Grader's Photo Essay, "How to Solve a Rubik's Cube"

	<u>Title page:</u> For this tutorial, we will be using the green face as a starting point in solving by forming the green cross. We will learn more about this step later. All algorithms are performed with the cube's front color facing you in the corresponding situation. The color of each face on the cube is determined by the color of the center piece.
	<u>Photo 1:</u> The Back Wedge, or B. Solving a Rubik's Cube is an intuitive and algorithmic process. One must use certain algorithms, or fixed sets of movements, to solve a cube. These algorithms are notated by the wedges of the cube. For example, B is the Back Wedge. Other possible wedges are Front or F, Left Wedge or L, Right Wedge or R, Up Wedge or U.
	<u>Photo 2:</u> The Down Wedge, or D. Movements are indicated by algorithms like this: RD'RD. The letter signifies which wedge to turn. The apostrophe means the wedge is turned counterclockwise. A letter by itself means the wedge is turned clockwise. For example the algorithm R'D'RD would involve turning the right face counterclockwise, the down face counter clockwise, the right face clockwise and the down face clockwise.
	<u>Photo 7:</u> The Scrambled Cube. Now, our first objective in solving the Rubik's Cube is to solve the green face. We will do this by inserting edge pieces (pieces with two colors on them as opposed to corner pieces, which have three) into their corresponding positions and lining up the color of each center with each piece. Okay, first step, identify edge pieces with green on them.
	<u>Photo 8:</u> This step is quite intuitive. Our goal is to get the green edge pieces, like the one in this photo, into the bottom face, match them with their corresponding center pieces, and move them back up to form a cross. The bottom, or opposite, face from green is blue, so we want to get the pieces there to line them up and to turn them to the green face.

(continued)

Figure 17. Excerpts From a Ninth Grader's Photo Essay, "How to Solve a Rubik's Cube" (*continued*)

	Photo 11: Now, to solve the green face by inserting corner pieces of a corresponding color scheme into the green face. See the green corner piece above? It is ready to be transferred to the top layer because it has a matching color scheme—green, white, orange—in the corner. The colors do not have to be in any particular order, just that they all are in the piece. To get the green piece up to the green face, here's your first algorithm: R'D'RD. Repeat it as many times as necessary to get the pieces into the correct position.
	Photo 13: If it was in this situation, with the corresponding color corner scheme in the bottom layer, it makes no difference. White, orange, green, okay, it's all good. Just do the same R'D'RD algorithm as many times as it takes until the piece is where it needs to be.
	Photo 16: We are matching corresponding color edges with their faces. Line up a colored edge with its corresponding center. In this case, it was yellow, red, with blue still on the top face. I lined up the yellow, red edge with the yellow center because the yellow part of the edge lines up with its corresponding color. We now have it matched, so we must get the red color on top of the yellow color on the edge to the left, to match it up and solve the gap. Holding the edge whose color is lined up with the center forward (example: yellow with yellow), do this algorithm: U'L'ULUFU'F', and that should solve it.
	Photo 27: Finally!!! The last step. And easy. It's just like putting in each corner of the cross in the beginning. We're just correctly putting each one corner into a correct orientation, solving the cube. Do R'D'RD on each piece you want until it reaches the top layer, then rotate the U face (Up) until another piece is in position to be put up. Do the R'D'RD algorithm and repeat this process until the cube is almost solved. (When doing this step, it appears you have messed up the cube, but if you stick to it, it will turn out fine.)
	Photo 29: Congratulations!!!!!!!!

the students who are behind begin to see others flaunt their photos, they will usually finish quickly.

Hand out the Photo Essay Evaluation handout and discuss the criteria with the class.

Next, students present their photo essays in front of the class on poster boards, in a notebook of photos and captions, or in a slide show with accompanying text for each slide. Once students have seen all class presentations, allow them to vote for the best three, using the Photo Essay Evaluation handout to "score" the presentations.

Below is a suggested timeline based on 50-minute, Monday through Friday classes:

- *2 weeks before due date:* Send letter about photo essays to parents.

- *1 week before due date:* Give students the assignment, show them superb examples of photo essays, give them some brief instruction on the operation of the camera, approve topics, and tell them the acceptable formats for presentation (notebook, poster board, or slide show).

- *2 or 3 days before due date:* Ask to see students' photographs. Do a demonstration lesson in which you mention aesthetics, page design, and typography. Show them effective models.

Enrichment

I originally designed Photo Essay as a way to bring expository or informative writing to life. However, the premise of combining image with text has multifarious possibilities. I have also assigned students the task of creating modern "Classics Illustrated" comic books from canonical works. After they have read a literary work, students enact scenes from the text, photograph the scenes, and add dialogue and explanatory text.

PHOTO ESSAY EVALUATION

Assign points for each item below, then total them up at the bottom:

_____ The presentation contains a minimum of 12 photos. (20 points)

_____ Photos are in focus, well lighted, sufficiently close up, relevant to the topic, and have good contrast. (20 points)

_____ Information is clearly written and easy to understand. The text uses precise and appropriate language. (20 points)

_____ The text describes the photos, but also extends the message beyond them. (20 points)

_____ The aesthetics of the presentation of the text and photos are pleasing. (20 points)

Total points: _____

From *Going Bohemian: How to Teach Writing Like You Mean It* (2nd edition) by Lawrence Baines & Anthony Kunkel. Copyright 2010 International Reading Association.

The Moody House: A Perspective Lesson for Creative Description

Type of Activity
Individual

Approximate Time
One or two 50-minute class periods

Objective
Students will learn to write from a variety of perspectives, demonstrate creative writing techniques, and incorporate the use of mood as a descriptive vehicle for writing.

Summary
It should be noted that this activity was adapted from several exercises in John Gardner's *The Art of Fiction* (1985).

The Moody House has been a turning point for students in class. Many students who make an effort on this activity will write something better and more creative than anything they have written before. The effectiveness of description through mood is a lesson that is learned well, and it is not uncommon for students to come in the next day and talk about how they did this with their friends or family once they got home. I make a point of reading some of the better descriptions out loud to the class, especially from those students who are very reluctant and tentative about their writing.

Materials
Paper and pen, photos of houses (in large books or PowerPoint), and an excerpt of effective, indirect writing

Setup
Have all materials on hand. I suggest using photos of the houses of famous writers (see Figure 18).

Figure 18. Photos of Famous Writers' Houses

Jane Austen

Ernest Hemingway

William Shakespeare

Stephen King

Charles Dickens

Edgar Allan Poe

Wallace Stevens

Procedure

Write the following excerpt from Arundhati Roy's (1997) *The God of Small Things* on the board:

> Despite the fact that it was June, and raining, the river was no more than a swollen drain now. A thin ribbon of thick water that lapped wearily at the mud banks on either side, sequined with the occasional silver slant of a dead fish. It was choked with a succulent weed, whose furred brown roots waved like thin tentacles underwater.

Discuss how the author charges the description with a sense of unease by using visuals such as *swollen, wearily, sequined with...dead fish,* and *tentacles*. The author did not write, "I am unhappy to be here. This place is ugly."

Show students your chosen photos of writers' homes. Have the students choose one house to write about. Once they have selected the house, give all students the following perspective to write from:

> You are happily married with two children. This morning you received news that members of your family have been seriously injured in a terrible plane crash. You are devastated. You feel empty, sad, confused, and a little angry.

Ask students to write at least a half page from this perspective and describe the house they have just imagined. When they write, they should offer "telling details" about the house (see the Show-Me Sentences activity on p. 52). They should be to communicate the description so vividly that the house is obvious to everyone in class. The idea is for each student to describe only the house, capturing the perspective character's sadness and sense of loss indirectly through description. At no time should the student use the first person "I" in their description or reveal any details about the perspective. The student should describe the house only, and in that description capture the feelings and emotions of the perspective from which they are writing.

When students are done writing, have them read aloud their descriptions one by one. After listening to each description, the rest of the class is polled to see which house they think the student is writing about. Ask students to offer a rationale about why they think it is a particular house. Highlight the telling details and particularly eloquent passages that convey misery through indirect description.

The second part of this activity is the same as the first, only you will ask students to open their minds and write from another perspective. Inform the students that they are standing in the same spot on the same road looking at the same house on the same day. This time, though, they are looking at the house from a different perspective:

> You have just gotten engaged. Your boss found out and gave you the promotion that you have been waiting for. You're excited about the future, you're happy, you're in love, and you've never had such a feeling of hope for the future.

Once again, instruct the students to describe the same house, only now their descriptions are to reflect joy. As with the depressed perspective, students should leave out personal details and concentrate on only describing the house. Offer students an example of how to transform perspective. You might say, "For instance, a swing set that formerly lay toppled and discarded, a vision of loss and abandonment, now could create an image of laughter, a vision of children to come, laughing and playing, a promise of hope for the future."

Have students read their new descriptions aloud and let other members of the class guess the house. Again, highlight the telling details and particularly descriptive passages that connote joy.

The final part of this activity is more for fun than any real educative value, but most students will want to try it. As they have done before, students should describe the same house, and again, they will write from a different perspective. This time students will write from the following perspective:

> You have just escaped from a mental institution. You are completely insane and view day-to-day interactions differently than a normal person would. Your worldview is warped and unreliable.

As they have been required to do in the previous descriptions, students should leave all mention of personal details out of their descriptions. The only indication to the reader of how demented the character is will be in the description of the house.

Enrichment

Follow this activity with another that is almost identical but personal to the students—make it relevant. Instruct students to think of something that happened in their lives that was important and then remember where it happened. Students should also try to remember how they felt while it was happening and write that feeling in one word, such as *happy, sad, angry, frightened,* or *excited.*

Once this is done, instruct them to describe the setting of that moment, writing nothing about their personal feelings but using descriptions of the setting to capture the emotion they felt. Follow this by reading aloud, or having the students read aloud, the descriptions and asking the class to guess the emotion that was being expressed.

RESOURCES

Gardner, J. (1985). *The art of fiction: Notes on craft for young writers.* New York: Vintage.

Roy, A. (1997). *The god of small things* (p. 118). New York: HarperCollins.

Ekphrasis for the Proletariat

Type of Activity
Individual

Approximate Time
One 50-minute class period

Objective
Students will consider the theme, tone, and narratives of several works of art, analyze some related poems, and write a poetic response.

Summary
Ekphrasis is art inspired by art, in this case, poetry inspired by paintings. A relatively obscure part of the curriculum, ekphrasis is generally associated with graduate study in literature and art. However, students of all ages find the range and diversity of artistic interpretations fascinating.

Materials
Copies of the Dædalus and Icarus handout (see p. 148), or copies of a retelling of this myth that is suitable for the students in your class, and copies of the Ekphrasis Poetry handout (see p. 149)

At a minimum, have three paintings to display. I suggest Pieter Bruegel's (c. 1558) *Landscape With the Fall of Icarus*, Henri Matisse's (1947) *Icarus*, and Herbert James Draper's (1898) *The Lament for Icarus*. All are available on the Internet and may be used free of charge for face-to-face teaching in the classroom (see the Resources section for URLs).

Music that refers to the myth of Daedelus and Icarus can be incorporated, too. Some possibilities include "Flight of Icarus" by Iron Maiden (Dickinson & Smith, 1983), "Daedalus" by Thrice (Breckenridge, Breckenridge, Kensrue, & Teranishi, 2008), "Too Close to the Sun" by Alan Parsons (Parsons, Bairnson, & Elliott, 1996), "Icarus" by Ani DiFranco (2003), and "Icarus" by Jason Webley (2004).

Setup

Bring in posters or display or print out artwork from the Internet that depicts the myth of Daedalus and Icarus. Make the art visible in the room or hand out full-color sheets to students.

Procedure

Discuss with students the paintings inspired by the myth of Icarus and Daedalus. Ask students to make predictions concerning what the story is going to be about. Compare the paintings by asking students to elucidate differences among them.

Pass out the Dædalus and Icarus handout. Read the story as a class. Discuss characterization, theme, and the moral lesson implied in the story.

Pass out the Ekphrasis Poetry handout. Students should read "Musée des Beaux Arts" by W.H. Auden (1938) silently, then read it aloud to each other in pairs. Help them understand the language and the plentiful allusions. Ask students to make observations about Bruegel's *Icarus* painting. Have them connect parts of Auden's poem to specific illustrations in Bruegel's painting. Discuss word selection, theme, and Auden's particular interpretation of the myth.

Next, have the students read William Carlos Williams's (1962) "Landscape With the Fall of Icarus." Follow the protocol established with the analysis of the Auden poem and Bruegel's painting. Compare the difference in focus between the poems by Auden and Williams.

Play some musical pieces that refer to Icarus or Daedalus, such as "Flight of Icarus" by Iron Maiden, "Daedalus" by Thrice, "Too Close to the Sun" by Alan Parsons, "Icarus" by Ani DiFranco, and "Icarus" by Jason Webley. Ask students to identify and interpret allusions in each song.

Enrichment

Students read another Greek myth, this time involving Apollo. Discuss the myth, then have students draw an image that relates to it. Finally, students create a poem based on their drawing in the style of Auden or Williams, or in another form. Students then present their drawings and read their poems aloud to the class.

After the presentations, consider studying Rainer Maria Rilke's (1908) poem "Archaic Torso of Apollo" along with one of the myriad sculptures or paintings that depict the Sun God. In actuality, Rilke wrote the poem after viewing a sculpture of the Sun God.

Some additional poems based on paintings include Edward Hirsch's (1986) "Edward Hopper and the House by the Railroad," X.J. Kennedy's (1985) "Nude Descending a Staircase," Henry Wadsworth Longfellow's (1870) "The Cross of Snow," and Frank O'Hara's (1957) "On Seeing Larry Rivers' *Washington Crossing the Delaware* at the Museum of Modern Art."

RESOURCES

Auden, W.H. (1938). *Musée des beaux arts* [Museum of fine arts]. Available at www.english.emory.edu/classes/paintings&poems/auden.html

Breckenridge, E., Breckenridge, R., Kensrue, D., & Teranishi, T. (2008). Daedalus (Recorded by Thrice). On *The alchemy index vols. III & IV: Air & earth* [CD]. Santa Monica, CA: Vagrant. Available at www.youtube.com/watch?v=wdkvdpn9KGA

Bruegel, P. (c. 1558). *Landscape with the fall of Icarus* [Painting]. Available at en.wikipedia.org/wiki/File:Bruegel,_Pieter_de_Oude_-_De_val_van_icarus_-_hi_res.jpg

Dickinson, B., & Smith, A. (1983). Flight of Icarus (Recorded by Iron Maiden). On *Piece of mind* [Album]. London: EMI. Available at www.youtube.com/watch?v=JKHku19fQck

DiFranco, A. (2003). Icarus. On *Evolve* [CD]. Buffalo, NY: Righteous Babe. Available at www.youtube.com/watch?v=yb7L2vDgxXw

Draper, H.J. (1898). *The lament for Icarus* [Painting]. Available at en.wikipedia.org/wiki/File:The_Lament_For_Icarus.jpg

Hirsch, E. (1986). *Edward Hopper and the house by the railroad*. Available at www.kunstpedia.com/articles/500/1/Edward-Hirsch-1950-poet-and-critic/Page1.html

Kennedy, X.J. (1985). *Nude descending a staircase*. Available at www.poemtree.com/poems/NudeDescendingAStaircase.htm

Longfellow, H.W. (1870). *The cross of snow*. Available at www.hwlongfellow.org/poems_poem.php?pid=205

Matisse, H. (1947). *Icarus* [Painting]. Available at www.artchive.com/artchive/M/matisse/icarus.jpg.html

O'Hara, F. (1957). *On seeing Larry Rivers'* Washington crossing the Delaware *at the Museum of Modern Art*. Available at www.poemhunter.com/poem/on-seeing-larry-rivers-washington-crossing-the-d/

Parsons, A., Bairnson, I., & Elliott, S. (1996). Too close to the sun (Recorded by Alan Parsons). On *On air* [CD]. Nashville, TN: River North. Available at www.youtube.com/watch?v=HTNyyaPFFXg

Rilke, R.M. (1908). *Archaic torso of Apollo*. Available at www.poemhunter.com/poem/archaic-torso-of-apollo/

Webley, J. (2004). Icarus. On *Only just beginning* [CD]. Seattle, WA: 11 Records. Available at www.youtube.com/watch?v=iMwa8Yq3ink

Williams, W.C. (1962). *Landscape with the fall of Icarus*. Available at www.poets.org/viewmedia.php/prmMID/15828

DÆDALUS AND ICARUS

Dædalus, a descendant of Erechtheus, was an Athenian architect, sculptor, and mechanician. He was the first to introduce the art of sculpture in its higher development, for before his time statues were merely rude representations, having the limbs altogether undefined.

But great as was his genius, still greater was his vanity, and he could brook no rival. Now his nephew and pupil, Talus, exhibited great talent, having invented both the saw and the compass, and Dædalus, fearing lest he might overshadow his own fame, secretly killed him by throwing him down from the citadel of Pallas-Athene. The murder being discovered, Dædalus was summoned before the court of the Areopagus and condemned to death; but he made his escape to the island of Crete, where he was received by King Minos in a manner worthy of his great reputation.

Dædalus constructed for the king the world-renowned labyrinth, which was an immense building, full of intricate passages, intersecting each other in such a manner, that even Dædalus himself is said, upon one occasion, to have nearly lost his way in it; and it was in this building the king placed the Minotaur, a monster with the head and shoulders of a bull and the body of a man.

In the course of time the great artist became weary of his long exile, more especially as the king, under the guise of friendship, kept him almost a prisoner. He therefore resolved to make his escape, and for this purpose ingeniously contrived wings for himself and his young son Icarus, whom he diligently trained how to use them. Having awaited a favourable opportunity, father and son commenced their flight, and were well on their way when Icarus, pleased with the novel sensation, forgot altogether his father's oft-repeated injunction not to approach too near the sun. The consequence was that the wax, by means of which his wings were attached, melted, and he fell into the sea and was drowned. The body of the unfortunate Icarus was washed up by the tide, and was buried by the bereaved father on an island which he called after his son, Icaria....

Dædalus passed the remainder of his life tranquilly in the island of Sicily, where he occupied himself in the construction of various beautiful works of art.

From *Myths and Legends of Ancient Greece and Rome* [e-book], by E.M. Berens, 2007, Project Gutenberg, p. 211, retrieved December 15, 2009, from www.gutenberg.org/files/22381/22381-h/22381-h.htm#page211.

EKPHRASIS POETRY

"Musée des Beaux Arts"
by W.H. Auden

About suffering they were never wrong,
The Old Masters; how well, they understood
Its human position; how it takes place
While someone else is eating or opening a
      window or just walking dully along;
How, when the aged are reverently, passionately
      waiting
For the miraculous birth, there always must be
Children who did not specially want it to happen,
      skating
On a pond at the edge of the wood:
They never forgot
That even the dreadful martyrdom must run its
      course
Anyhow in a corner, some untidy spot
Where the dogs go on with their doggy life and
      the torturer's horse
Scratches its innocent behind on a tree.

In Breughel's Icarus, for instance: how everything
      turns away
Quite leisurely from the disaster; the ploughman
      may
Have heard the splash, the forsaken cry,
But for him it was not an important failure; the
      sun shone
As it had to on the white legs disappearing into
      the green
Water; and the expensive delicate ship that must
      have seen
Something amazing, a boy falling out of the sky,
had somewhere to get to and sailed calmly on.

"Landscape With the Fall of Icarus"
by William Carlos Williams

According to Brueghel
when Icarus fell
it was spring

a farmer was ploughing
his field
the whole pageantry

of the year was
awake tingling
near

the edge of the sea
concerned
with itself

sweating in the sun
that melted
the wings' wax

unsignificantly
off the coast
there was

a splash quite unnoticed
this was
Icarus drowning

Creativity: Developing Creativity in Noncreative Types

We have to recognize imagination as a form of knowledge or our speculative fiction would vanish. Writers invent people they've never met, events that never happened, and countries that never existed.

But if your fiction is to live, something deeply immediate and personal must be at its heart.

From *Making Shapely Fiction* by Jerome Stern

It's been too long since you've *given* a creative writing assignment. Lately, you feel as if the focus on test prep and reading comprehension has taken your classes hostage. It seems that every time you begin to plan something, you panic and find yourself teaching something else. There is the *test* that always lies ahead.

The school's focus is last year's scores, the school's performance, and which students should be on your radar for the upcoming *test*. The writing expectations have become formulaic. Tone and voice are second to focus and organization. You're aware that those who are creative, gifted, or inspired suffer in this setting, but those who point their fingers at education expect a tolerable average, and in this climate, it is the inspired who are taken for granted. They will test well regardless, and mediocrity is acceptable for them.

The problem is that you're not "on board" with the reforms, and you've been accused of deviating from your expected path before. You know that you can teach these kids to reach, to surprise themselves with their own words, but it is not a formula that is measurable by means and deviations, and it does not fit well within the definition of a standard essay. It has become frustrating for both you and your students. Time moves on, and you have not covered half the material you had set out to teach and have not had the fun in the classroom you had promised yourself this year.

Your literature text has some decent short stories in it, and with any luck, you might be able to create a few short assignments from one of them. Still, the school has a new reading coach, and you are expected to document your attempts at teaching reading comprehension. You thumb through the text, noting which stories could be used for dissection and discussion. The stories have themes and elements that could be useful, but you also know that most of your students will check out once the reading discussions begin. That leaves the inevitable questions at the end of the story for them to work on. Nothing too new or exciting there, but the reading coach will be satisfied.

As you place the textbook flat on your desk, you smile. You realize it's time for a gut check. You could simply do the readings, do the recommended writing, and sadly enough, you would be praised for doing what you're expected to do. Instead, you decide that perhaps it's time to break with the standardized expectation and focus on having these kids actually experience what it means to discuss writing with authority. Perhaps this unit on short stories could be addressed from a slightly more creative angle.

The bell rings and students shuffle to their seats. Many pull out their books, settle in, and stare at you, waiting for the assignment and page number. You smile warmly at the class and mumble, "No textbooks today."

With these few words, you have momentarily engaged your students. You had almost forgotten what it felt like to have the attention of the entire class. "Everybody, get out a sheet of paper and something to write with," you say. You turn to the board and write the numbers 1 and 5, one on top of the other. The students are looking at you with interest. You point to the numbers. "I'm going to write a story, and these are my two characters." You pause and smile again. "Pick two numbers between 1 and 5 and write them just as I have. We'll see who you get to invent."

The Poignant Page:
A Focused Approach to Microfiction

Type of Activity
Individual

Approximate Time
Two 50-minute class periods

Objective
Students will write succinctly and with purpose, and demonstrate knowledge of tone and voice.

Summary
Microfiction—also termed flash fiction, poetic fiction, and other names—is a growing art form in writing. I like to attach the idea of understatement to the story, because it has worked well in helping the students write something important, or poignant. Many high school students live in a world of drama and exaggeration. To ask them to consciously create meaning without being direct is a new experience for them.

   Some will do okay, but others will create something beautiful, and when they do, writing will never be the same for them. Figure 19 contains a piece written by a former student. Laura was a good student, but she hadn't written anything that had resonated with her or the class. Structure and formula were what she did best, and the story she wrote for this assignment was a challenge, but with this story, I believe she captured the idea beautifully.

Materials
Pen and paper, or a computer with a word-processing program, and copies of the "Wanting to Fly" by Stephen Dunning handout (see p. 157)

Figure 19. A Student's Poignant Page

"Guilt of a Killer" by Laura Neylan:

It was a beautiful summer day, but Katie wouldn't see it. A ray of sunlight came in through the window and fell across her stomach. Instead of allowing the sun to warm her, she leapt out of bed. Making her way to the kitchen, the aroma of eggs tempted her lips to break in a smile. But Katie was resilient in her despondence. Katie's mother was humming a tune over the stove and called out, "Good morning, baby," as her daughter approached.

Katie stopped in her tracks as disbelief, anger, and regret flooded through her veins. How could this woman, a mother, be so inherently insensitive? Katie quickly turned around and stormed out of the front door.

The rays of sunshine made her skin tingle and her hair shine, but she didn't notice. She walked along the sidewalk, staring at her toes. Katie found her way to the neighborhood park where she heard the gleeful shouts of children. Glancing up from the ground, she watched as a group of kids played soccer. Instinctively, Katie felt a sharp kick in her stomach. But it was only a memory.

Setup

Microfiction is not a new idea, so there are plenty of examples on the Internet to share with the students. Spend some time discussing the idea of a microfiction story with the class. For this assignment, it's helpful to discuss what it means to write an entire story on one page of paper. The idea of a story in one page is to tell as much about a person or a life as possible within a short amount of writing. Where a typical story may focus on plot and conflict, the one-page story will focus on letting the reader make the conclusions that will create the story. Also, a review of tone and mood in writing will prove helpful to many students.

Procedure

Begin this assignment with a short lesson on understatement. Write the term on the board and write the following definition:

> Understatement is a figure of speech where the writer reduces the importance or significance of something that is actually significant.

With this definition on the board, ask the students to clarify the definition.

Next write a literary example on the board, such as,

> He adds a further touch by telling her that he is going home for an operation: "It isn't very serious. I have this tiny little tumor on the brain."
> (From *The Catcher in the Rye*, by J.D. Salinger, Boston: Little, Brown, p. 59.)

With the example on the board, ask the students to take out a piece of paper and see if they can write an understatement of their own. Oftentimes at this point, some of the students will actually write a hyperbole, and that is a good opportunity to discuss understatement as something considered to be the opposite of an exaggeration. Many students will find it difficult to create an understatement, so once you see that a student has done so successfully, ask him or her to read it aloud. For instance, one student of mine wrote,

> When our family was on vacation, our reservation was mixed up, so they upgraded us to a two-room suite. When they took us up to the room, my father said, "I guess it will do." It was the nicest room any of us had ever seen.

This was a good example for the class, because not only did it put a context to the understatement, but also the sentence following the understatement was exactly the type of writing I would be asking them to do.

After a discussion on understatement, tell the class that they will be writing a microfiction story. Instruct them that they are to write a story that takes only one page of writing or less and that they should focus on two things:

1. Stories need to use understatement, whether direct or implied.
2. Stories need to have a bigger meaning with regard to what's *not* said.

For an example of this, pass out and ask students to read the microfiction story handout "Wanting to Fly" by Stephen Dunning (1996). This story encompasses an entire lifetime through understatement and the implications of what is said. It is a good example of what's expected.

Enrichment

Once the stories are finished, a nice follow-up is to spend a class reading them. For this, I have all the students make enough copies of their stories for the whole class, and each student gets a copy from all of their peers. Weather permitting, I take the kids outside and let them find a tree or bench to sit and read. When we come back in the room, the feedback and sharing is pretty amazing, as well as enjoyable.

RESOURCE
Dunning, S. (1996). "Wanting to fly." In J. Stern (Ed.), *Micro fiction: An anthology of really short stories* (pp. 46–47). New York: W.W. Norton.

"WANTING TO FLY" BY STEPHEN DUNNING

At the State Fair a man in silver tights and handlebar mustache—some name like The Great Zambini—blasts from a cannon. Driving home, Father calls me "Goosey Zamboosi" and "Flying Weenie." But later, when I spray my BVDs with Ma's birdcage paint, he paddles me good.

Again.

For my ninth birthday, ma gives me a silver-gray T-shirt with Halley's Comet flashing across. I can fly in that shirt—arms stiff, tilting. Then Mrs. McKissup catches us on the kindergarten slide. "You boys! Let the children use it."

In two minutes Duncan and me're in Beaver's office.

"Childish," Mr. Beaver says. "Selfish." Duncan giggles. "What would you do, you're trying to run a decent school?" We both giggle.

Father uses the hairbrush.

Duncan and me nail a refrigerator carton to the Frenzels' porch roof. Duncan falls awful hard, grabbing his ankle. "It's broke," he hollers. I run for his ma. Next rain the Frenzels' roof sprinkles like a watering can.

My last beating ever.

Wallace's Carnival hires me to assemble rides—dollar a day, food, sleep anywhere I can. We head for Toledo, Willie Farley driving the ferris-wheel truck. It's Willie teaches me cannon-flying. I get pretty famous.

Then of course Father and me get along. I'm home from Cole Brothers when Father drowns, ice-fishing with Arn Bower. Before they hook him, I see his face—mouth open and lopsided, a giant perch.

Arn Bower starts keeping Ma company, and that's good. There's women wherever I fly.

From "Wanting to Fly," by S. Dunning, 1996, in J. Stern (Ed.), *Micro Fiction: An Anthology of Really Short Stories*, pp. 46–47, New York: W.W. Norton.

Pensive Pirates:
A Creative Activity on Character, Plot, Conflict, and Red Herrings

Type of Activity
Individual

Approximate Time
Four 50-minute class periods

Objective
Students will develop characters and conflicts, and identify red herrings within their writing.

Summary

This assignment is an adaptation of an old activity I was given many years ago for which we were asked to combine prescribed characters into a story. I've experimented with many characters of my own invention over the years and have found that the five characters presented here work well with young teens. Having said that, you are completely capable of swapping out all of the characters and conflicts for this assignment with your own inventions.

Pensive Pirates is a great assignment for students after they have done either a long, more traditional assignment or when you wish to work on such elements as descriptive writing, tone, and literary elements. Students will often seem a bit stunned with the introduction of the assignment, but most will enjoy the challenge. It is helpful to discuss the characters a bit and ask students to consider how they will introduce them with their unique attributes. Some will simply wish to restate that which is written on the handout, but I often challenge them to create a scene for the introduction of each character that *shows* the character being who they are.

Materials

Pen and paper, or a computer with a word-processing program, and copies of the Pensive Pirates Creative Writing Story Assignment handout (see p. 162)

Setup

Either on the chalkboard, overhead, or in a handout, provide the following definitions (or other definitions of your preference) to the students:

- *Characterization:* The author expresses a character's personality through the use of action, dialogue, thought, or commentary by the author or another character.
- *Secondary characters:* These characters can make or break a story. They bring in the texturing that colors the line of your hero's or heroine's character. They can be mirrors, foils, instigators, protectors, fall guys, scapegoats, cheerleaders, misdirectors—the list goes on and on.
- *Conflict:* This is the struggle within the story: character divided against self, character against character, character against society, character against nature, character against God. Without it, there is no story.
- *Red herring:* In literature, a red herring is a narrative element intended to distract the reader from a more important event in the plot, usually a twist ending.

Discuss the terms and definitions with the students, providing examples when possible.

Procedure

These procedures will follow the format I use for this assignment, although you may wish to allow students the opportunity to choose from the varied characters and conflicts. The characters and conflicts for this assignment will be provided at the end of this procedure section.

Inform the students that they will be creating a story that will call on their grasp of the terms that have just been covered. It's fun for the students if the assignment is set up with an element of luck and randomness to the characters and conflicts, but it's not necessary.

Tell students to take out a piece of paper and write down any two numbers between 1 and 5, one on top of the other. Then, instruct students to select one letter between A and D and write that letter below their two numbers. At this point, all students should have two numbers and one letter written on their papers.

Now you'll want to read aloud the characters and conflicts. Tell the students that they are locked into the characters and conflicts they will be creating, however they correspond to their numbers and letters. Inform them that the two numbers they selected will be their primary character and secondary character (I allow the students the choice to decide who is primary and who is secondary). Read the numbers and character descriptions one by one, asking the students to write the names of their assigned characters next to their numbers. Explain that they'll be provided a handout with the descriptions, so all they need to write is the names.

When all students have been assigned a primary and secondary character (numbers 1–5), inform them that their letter (A–D) will be the conflict that takes place within their stories—the problem that must be resolved within the story. Read the letters and conflict descriptions aloud and tell students to write their conflicts next to their numbers.

All students should now have two characters and a conflict for their stories. Last, inform the students that their stories must also include a red herring. This is a bit comical, but over the years, I've found the idea of an inept pirate to work well for the red herring.

At this point, I give the Pensive Pirates Creative Writing Story Assignment handout to the students so that they may see the full assignment. I allow them the period to brainstorm, discuss red herrings, expectations, descriptions, and so forth, and begin writing. For this assignment, I allow two periods of in-class writing, a third period for peer critiques and revisions, then have volunteer presentations during the fourth period. Figure 20 contains an excerpt from a recent student piece.

Enrichment
This is a great assignment to follow up with some focused descriptive writing. Completing the Show-Me Sentences lesson (see p. 52) before this

Figure 20. Excerpt From a Student's Pensive Pirates Writing

The susurrations of the forest marked the time as we strolled. Jilly occasionally performed parkour-like jumps and flips off the sturdy trees and outcrops of rock, her leonine impulses allowing her to land safely despite the apparent danger. Abruptly, on the verge of performing yet another acrobatic feat, she stiffened and wheeled around, her mien speaking of strained alertness. Pausing, I heard it. A soft lowing floated out amid the trees. A flash of clairvoyance—we simultaneously darted toward the receding calls. The distressed creature cried out frantically, spurring us onward.

We shot through a decrepit fence into dazzling sunlight, blearily looking around, wondering where—

"GET BACK, WENCHES, OR I'LL RUN YE THROUGH!"

The harsh voice lacerated the tremulous breeze. We spun left just in time to avoid the eye patch, peg leg, and broadsword of our attacker. Realization struck us. The distressed sounds had been the lowings of the pygmy cow upon which the pirate perched. We jumped clear again as the pirate spurred the poor creature toward us.

Before he could turn, Jilly sharply kicked him off his mount. Overjoyed at its deliverance, the pygmy cow avenged itself. The pirate soon lay flat on his face, completely floored by the dazzling array of martial arts displayed by the quadruped. She might have been small, but that bovine kicked like a stallion.

assignment allows you the opportunity to target revision for description. Students can identify telling sentences within character description and turn these into more developed scenes, or moments, within their writing.

Typically, after writing these stories, many students will wish for the opportunity to share them. Depending on time, it is fun for the students to have that forum to hear or read the stories of their peers.

Another idea that I have done is to have the students follow this assignment with a second one that requires the students to turn their red herrings into a stand-alone story. It's not uncommon for the red herring to dominate one of the pensive pirate stories, and the product that comes from this second assignment is often more clever and natural in tone than the original one.

PENSIVE PIRATES
CREATIVE WRITING STORY ASSIGNMENT

Your task will be to write a short story that focuses on using all of the literary elements described below. You have already selected two numbers to determine who your primary and secondary characters will be, as well as a letter for the main conflict within your story.

Primary and secondary characters that must appear in your stories:
Your invented character is to be the primary character within your story. As your story progresses, this character should become more developed. You must use the numbers you already selected, but it is up to you to decide who is primary and who is secondary.

1. Cosmo is a 15-year-old male wannabe skateboarder who insists on jumping over everything he sees.

2. Rolo is a 10-year-old boy who is a compulsive whiner and extremely out of shape.

3. Jilly is a 14-year-old girl and nationally ranked gymnast who is a complete and total control freak.

4. Tilly is a 17-year-old girl who is a complete tree hugging, earth loving, hippie chick.

5. Stanley is a 16-year-old male who is deaf and has a severe case of narcolepsy.

Primary conflicts that must be introduced, escalated, and resolved within your stories:

A. A sinking boat

B. A stolen cow

C. A kaleidoscope

D. An angry squirrel

Finally, all stories must include a dysfunctional, or pensive, pirate (as in a bad pirate) as a red herring.

Do your best to write an intriguing story that develops your primary character, involves your secondary character, builds a conflict, and includes a red herring. There's a good deal of thinking that needs to be done to create and combine these literary items, but you should also have some fun with your writing as you create and bring events to life.

From *Going Bohemian: How to Teach Writing Like You Mean It* (2nd edition) by Lawrence Baines & Anthony Kunkel. Copyright 2010 International Reading Association.

Three Ways of Looking at Me

Type of Activity
Individual

Approximate Time
One 50-minute class period

Objective
Students will use descriptive language to describe themselves now, five years ago, and five years hence.

Summary
Three Ways of Looking at Me helps students develop their descriptive and observational skills, and encourages them to analyze where they have been and where they are going. This activity is usually successful with a range of students, because it involves close analysis of something that students find endlessly fascinating—themselves.

Materials
Pens and paper, and a set of hand mirrors

Setup
Tell students to look at themselves in a hand mirror and write a physical description of themselves.

Procedure
Students should provide at least three analogies for how they look as well as a list of activities that they enjoy, using action verbs. Finally, they need to write and explain three current goals or obsessions.

   Next, ask students to imagine themselves looking in a mirror five years ago. They should follow the procedure already established: writing a physical description, at least three analogies, a list of activities they enjoyed, and three goals or obsessions that they had at the time. Finally, students imagine themselves looking in a mirror five years hence and complete the writing based on their future vision of themselves: a physical description, at least three analogies, a list of activities they enjoy, and three goals or obsessions. As a culminating activity, have students write a paper contrasting themselves over time, as demonstrated by Courtney's writing in Figure 21.

Figure 21. Three Ways of Looking at Me: Courtney

Physical description:
I have an alien head. For some reason, my head is larger than the rest of my body. Considering that my nose is ginormous, one might think the largeness of my head would offset the undeniable largeness of my nose, but it doesn't. Where did I get this nose, one might wonder? From my Cherokee ancestors who passed it down from Great-Grandma Rogers. Could they have given me any other trait from my Native American heritage like beautiful dusky skin that all the boys seem to drool over? Nope. Instead, I get porcelain skin, high cheek bones, thin lips, and sharp features that reflect the Euro-Anglo side of my family. Thanks, Grandma, for intermingling with "the White Man."

Okay, I digress. My eyes are the color of muddy water. I guess some people call them hazel, but they're mostly a deep, murky green. I have small eyes. I wish they were bigger, but it doesn't help that they are hidden behind a pair of thick, blue-rimmed glasses that correct my nearsighted vision. By the time I put these coke bottles on, my eyes look like little beads that could disappear at any moment. And, I haven't gotten to my hair, yet. < Sigh > What was I thinking when I put in that sun-in hair color? It was supposed to turn my brunette locks a rich, golden blonde that promised to drive the boys wild, but what did I get? A rich, golden orange that resembled a pumpkin. Nice.

Activities:
Luckily, my slender frame is good for all of the sports I play. I'm average height, but I'm pretty quick, which allows me to be the starting point guard for our basketball team. I'm not really into basketball; I play more for my mom because she wants me to get a scholarship, but, really, I hate it. I just use it to condition for track season. I'm the anchor leg on all of the relay teams. Somehow I'm a sprinter and a distance runner at the same time. I like track because, other than the relays, it's an individual sport. I don't like people counting on me to win or lose—too much pressure. Besides, I don't really like people. This is a bit ironic since I'm usually the life of the party. I have a lot of friends, and my social calendar is booked, but I really prefer to be alone reading a book. Sometimes, when I want to disappear, I go to the bushes that grow against the side of my house; I'll crawl behind them and spend hours reading. Since I'm involved in every social club,

(continued)

Figure 21. Three Ways of Looking at Me: Courtney (*continued*)

academic club, and extracurricular sport available, it's kind of nice enjoying the silence. I don't have to be "on."

Goals:
In five years, I want to graduate high school in the top ten percent and have a full ride to college, since my parents can't afford to send me. I want to major in communications and become a news anchor. I'd really like to go to OSU, but it depends on scholarship money. I do not want to be tied down. My only current obsession is Brad, who is the hottest guy [in school]. God smiled down on me when he placed our lockers side-by-side this year. Now, if I can just get him to realize I'm alive, we might have a chance.

Courtney @ 8: Physical/activities/goals:
I look like my brother. He's two years older than I am, but he's small for his age, and someone asked us the other day if we were twins. I knew I shouldn't have cut my hair short, but Dad didn't give me a choice when he said it had to be short enough that I couldn't chew on it. In my defense, I only chew on it when I'm nervous. He just happens to be paying attention at the wrong time. Oh well, it's not like I even like combing it anyway. It's this wiry, dirty brown color. Mom tries to curl it for school pictures, and she just makes me look like an old lady. She seems to think volume makes everything look better when she's really just using it as an excuse to make me look like a girl. I hate looking like a girl. I hate bows. I hate pink. I hate frills. I hate dresses. And, god, don't even try to get me to wear panty hose. Who the hell invented that torture? They're so binding! Give me a good pair of jeans and a comfy T-shirt and I'm happy. I know my Mom wishes I was more feminine, but I'd rather climb trees, ride my bike, wrestle with my brother, and play sports. I don't even like taking baths. I mean, I can't smell myself, so it must not be time to wash.

Let's see, I already said I looked like my brother, but let me go into a little more detail. I'm super skinny and I'm missing half of my teeth because they all seemed to fall out at the same time. My complexion is an olive color from spending all of my time playing outside. I look like the basic tomboy—nothing significant. In fact, I really don't notice my looks much because I don't care. All of my girlfriends seem to be boy crazy, and they make me want to gag. I mean, boys are fun to play kickball and stuff, but to date? Gross!!! In fact, I'm pretty good buddies with most of the boys at my school, and they fight over whose team I'm on when we're in P.E. All of the girls want to be cheerleaders, but who wants to do something stupid like that? Boooooring! It's more fun being in the mix, and showing the boys that I'm just as good as they are (usually better) when we're playing soccer or whatever.

What are my goals? I want to steal the soccer ball from Delano at recess. He's the best player, and, if I can stuff him, I'll show those boys that I'm one of them. I also want to have perfect attendance. My school gives a special medal to students who come to school every day, and that would be really cool! My third goal is to win the art contest this year. I've won every one I've entered so far, and I want to keep the streak going. Besides, they're giving a $50 savings bond to the winner, and that's a lot of money!

(continued)

Figure 21. Three Ways of Looking at Me: Courtney (*continued*)

Courtney @ 18:

Well, I hope I grow into my nose. I mean, I heard that the head is the first thing to reach adult size, so, hopefully, my melon will proportion itself out. If I could just equalize the size of those two things, I'll look halfway decent. I'm trading in these glasses for contacts, but Mom won't let me get colored lenses; so, I have to stick with my muddy water eye color. I've started wearing makeup, which helps my attractiveness a little bit, but my features are still pretty sharp since I'm so thin. I still have porcelain skin, thin lips, high cheek bones, and a gonzo schnoz. My hair resembles the fiery red of leaves that change in the beginning of autumn. This color fits my pale complexion, and most people think it's my natural color. (I like it because it makes me different. I hate looking like everyone else.) I wear it to my shoulders so that people don't think I'm a boy since I still look a lot like my brother. I wear bangs because I read in a beauty magazine that this helps reduce the image of one's nose. (Can you tell I'm obsessed?) Not sure if it's true, but it helps me get through the day. My clothes aren't really trendy because my family doesn't have a lot of money to spend on things like that. I don't really have a sense of style, and I still don't care all that much. I'm still a tomboy at heart, but I'm trying to be a little more feminine. I'm not sure why. I guess it's because it's what I'm supposed to do.

I'm kind of taking an indefinite break from basketball and track. I was able to pacify my Mom by going out for cross country instead. I love running. I love hearing my breath labor as I run past the first mile...then the second...the third...the fourth.... It gives me time to think. I don't have to talk to anyone, and the only sound is my feet crunching through leaves and gravel as I make my way through the course. I can run as hard or as light as I want to. I like to deceive people by pacing myself during races, and staying thirteen people behind until the very end when I sprint the last 200 meters and blow them away. Luckily, I'm the team captain, which keeps my Mom off of my back about quitting the other sports. She was really hoping I'd get an athletic scholarship, and she feels as though I'm wasting my talent, but she kind of sucked the fun out of it for me. But, hey, what are Moms for? She says I'm too stubborn and strong-willed, which might have something to do with my decision to become a borderline feminist.

Unfortunately, Brad never worked out, but I've dated enough to know that boys are retarded. I'd rather spend my time alone reading a good book than listening to them talk about themselves. Besides, boyfriends just hold a girl back. I have things I want to do in my life, and I don't want to get tied down. That's why I'm still involved in every school club and community organization. I have to build that transcript and resume to ensure my future.

My goals are to attend Cameron University on the full ride I just obtained, and graduate in four years with a B.A. in English. This is a big deal because I'd be a first-generation college graduate, and I will have done it all on my own. After I get my bachelor's, I want to get my master's and doctorate because I want to be a college professor. I also want to travel. I know I want to go to England, but I think it would be cool to go to Italy, too. I want to see the world and change lives. Maybe I could do a foreign exchange student thing when I get to college since my Mom never would let me in high school.

Enrichment

Three Ways of Looking at Me would be enhanced if students could bring an old photo of themselves to work off of for the second piece of writing (description of themselves five years ago). The piece on the future could be enhanced with interviews with friends, teachers, or family.

Another strength of Three Ways of Looking at Me is its applicability with English-language learners. Because the exercise requires self-examination in the present tense, reflection about the past, and prognostication about the future, students use their own language as a basis from which to write. The delineations among present, past, and future also help establish the patterns for verbs to indicate when an event occurred.

Creating Man: A Formula for Character

Type of Activity
Individual

Approximate Time
One 50-minute class period

Objective
Students will learn how to create fictional characters, develop creative writing skills, and understand character development in writing.

Summary
This lesson has had remarkable success in all of my classes. If possible, read the students' character sentences aloud and talk about the depth created with the description and thoughts of the characters. The formula, if followed, will always read well, and the students will enjoy hearing the quality they have produced.

The step-by-step, sentence-by-sentence approach to creating a character is one that even the most reluctant of students will pick up easily, and the quality of the characters many of them create will surprise and engage them. What I find generally happens in my class is that many of the students will realize that they have created a short piece of quality fiction that they did not realize they were capable of writing, and this realization leads to a willing class full of engaged students.

Materials
Pen and paper

Setup
None

Procedure

This activity is best done in two parts: first, the creation of a character, then the description.

Part 1

Instruct all students that they will be creating a character and will need a piece of paper and something to write with. Table 1 shows each step of the first part of the lesson, and you'll need to model an example for the students with each step, one sentence at a time. With each step described in the following text, I give a sentence example in Table 1 that you can use in class.

First, instruct students to use their imagination and invent a character by giving it a first name and a last name. Then, using one sentence only, each student is to write his or her character's full name on the paper and follow it with a sentence in which the character does something that shows action.

Second, they are to give their characters a thought. Have students add the following sentence to their first one: [Fill in the blank], he [or she] thought.

Next, instruct students to add one more sentence that begins with a pronoun and shows their characters in active action (as opposed to passive action).

Table 1. Step-by-Step Instructions and Examples for Part 1 of the Creating Man Activity

Formula	Sentence Example
1. [Character's full name + action verb + rest of sentence	Jane Doe took hold of the chainsaw.
2. [Fill in the blank,] + "he [or she] thought."	I wonder how messy this will be, she thought.
3. Pronoun beginning active action sentence	She opened the door softly and stepped quietly into the room.
4. Memory or thought about the past	She thought of her last husband and a time when her life had been much simpler.
5. Action sentence that concludes the scene	Jane moved quietly to the edge of the bed where the man lay sleeping, then smiling coldly, she pulled the cord and brought the chainsaw to life.

Now tell students to add another sentence, giving their characters a memory or thought about the past.

Finally, have students write one last sentence that shows action and concludes the scene they have written thus far.

Part 2

Once all students have concluded their character scenes, begin the description formula for their characters. This part of the activity will focus on giving physical description through action to their newly invented characters. To help avoid confusion, it is best to inform students that the descriptions they are about to write have nothing to do with the scenes they have just created, except for the fact that they are each using their same character—same character, different scene. Table 2 shows each step of the second part of the lesson, with example sentences for the students.

First, have each student write his or her character's full name, followed by "stood in front of the mirror." This will be the first sentence of the description.

Then, instruct students to follow the first sentence with a descriptive sentence about their characters. It's helpful to explain to the class that their characters are now looking at themselves in the mirror and should notice something that helps describe them physically.

Table 2. Step-by-Step Instructions and Examples for Part 2 of the Creating Man Activity

Formula	Sentence Example
1. [Character's full name] + "stood in front of the mirror."	Jane Doe stood in front of the mirror.
2. A physically descriptive sentence	The wrinkles around her eyes seemed deeper than she remembered.
3. Pronoun beginning descriptive sentence	She lifted a trembling hand to her short, dark hair.
4. [Fill in the blank,] + "he [or she] thought."	Where has the time gone, she thought.
5. Concluding action and character leaving mirror	She lowered her hand, shook her head sadly, and walked away from the mirror.

Third, tell students to begin the next sentence of their description with the proper pronoun for their characters and finish it with some descriptive action. Have their characters do something that will tell something about their looks.

Next, have students give their characters a thought using only one sentence: [Fill in the blank,] + "he [or she] thought."

Last, each student should write an action sentence in which his or her character either leaves the mirror or breaks it.

Enrichment

An idea that works well in conjunction with Creating Man is following the activity with a short-story assignment. I ask students to write short stories using the characters they have created in their Creating Man sentences. I have found that this increases the quality of the stories that are written and makes them much more personal to the students who are writing them.

Formatting the Story: Focusing on Setting, Character, and Plot

Type of Activity
Group

Approximate Time
Five 50-minute class periods

Objective
Students will learn to identify and discuss setting, character, and plot within a short story, demonstrate descriptive and creative writing techniques, demonstrate rewording and revision skills, create characters for fictional writing, and write plot and setting treatments for short stories.

Summary
Some of my students' best descriptive writing has been produced during this activity, and most of my students finish this lesson knowing more about the short story than they would have with any amount of book work. Within a group activity, the students become easily motivated and often can be seen together agonizing and arguing over different ways to best word a particular phrase or description.

Materials
Creative pictures or paintings will be needed, one for each group or individual, as the case may be. In the past, I have used various covers from *The New Yorker* or other magazines, always with the titles cut off. Art transparencies also work. Basically, you'll need a colorful visual that can stimulate a large number of stories from the students.

You'll also need copies of the Formatting Your Story handout (see p. 176).

Setup

Select a short story that can be read in one class period with time left for a short discussion. The story is intended primarily as a means to demonstrate setting, character, and plot.

Procedure

Day 1

Read the short story you selected, leaving enough time for a short discussion afterward.

Once the story is read, discuss its setting, character(s), and plot, focusing specifically on what these elements of story are and any piece of the story that may have exemplified them well. It is opportune to introduce conflict and resolution during an explanation of plot. I have made it a habit to tell my students that plot in a short story is "the sequence of events and the conflict and resolution that take place within a story."

Day 2

After a short recap of setting, character, and plot, divide the students into groups of three or four and hand out the creative pictures in random order. To make the activity fun, put the pictures in a paper bag and have a member from each group reach in and pull one out.

Then, instructed the groups to look at their picture and discuss the story that is inside it. Instruct them to think in terms of setting, character, and plot, and decide where and when the story takes place, who the main character of the story is, and the story's plot. Also, the groups should discuss the conflict of the story and how it will be resolved. At this point, refer to the story read the previous day and again briefly discuss its setting, characters, and plot.

About 10 minutes later, when the groups have settled in and begun developing some ideas, give them the Formatting Your Story handout.

Once all groups have had a chance to go over the handouts and all questions regarding the assignment have been answered, it's time to get to work. Require that once groups start writing, every group member has a chance to write. How the groups split up the work is up to them, but all members must do equal writing.

Note: It helps to give students daily expectations and deadlines to ensure they stay on task and don't waste time. For this assignment, it is normal for much of the explanation and setup to take a good portion of the class, so I ask that each group only begin their writing and have something to show by the end of the period. Also, because this is an in-class assignment, all groups should leave their format work with you, along with their pictures and the instructional handouts.

Day 3

Hand out the in-progress formats to their respective groups and allow students to commence work. This is a good day to monitor their progress and assist any students who are struggling with the intensity of the writing assignment. Typically, you should require all groups to complete their formats on this day. These are actually only rough drafts, so allow them to sacrifice spelling, punctuation, and neatness to complete the formats within the time frame allowed. Encourage students to use a thesaurus while they write.

For the faster groups that tend to finish too early, you can allow them to read a short story, or you could go over weaknesses in their formats that they may wish to spend some time on for the rest of the class period.

Once again, it is best to collect all work before the students leave.

Day 4

This is revision day. Most groups should have completed their formats by now, but those who may be lagging behind will have a chance to catch up today. Hand out the format drafts to the groups and instruct each group to separate the setting, character, and plot, and then divide the elements among their group. Instruct students to make sure they have a paper in front of them other than the one that they did all (or most) of the writing on.

Once all students have their assigned formats, they are instructed to do a complete revision on the paper they have in front of them. Changes, rewording, adding synonyms, deleting, adding description, spelling, and grammar checks should be mandatory. (I instruct those students who are unsure of what's expected that for every three sentences written, they should make changes or additions to at least one.)

Once group members have completed their revisions, they are to pass their papers to the left (within their group) and repeat the process on the paper that's being passed to them. All group members will wind up doing a complete revision on all pages written within their groups, including their own.

Note: It is effective in this part of the activity for you to actually sit down with some of the groups and join the revision process. I often sit with a group and rewrite a sentence or two of theirs, usually using some colorful adjectives. This helps some of the students see firsthand exactly what is expected in their revisions.

Collect all papers at the end of class.

Day 5

Hand out the papers to their respective groups. Give students the entire class period to finish revising their formats and writing polished copies of them on clean sheets of paper. Each group member should take turns on each paper, as they did the day before, and make sure to wind up with his or her original paper about 10 minutes before the end of the class period. All revisions from the previous day should be included on their final copies, and all spelling and grammar errors should be corrected.

The final product should be written neatly, with each member of the group having done his or her part in the rewriting of the final copy. Instruct students to give their final formats a title and include a title page—the more colorful the better. I usually require the rough drafts to be turned in with final copies and include the revisions done on them in the grading process.

Enrichment

Once all of the formats are done, there are several things that can be done with them. One idea that has worked well in my classes is to redistribute the formats, making sure no group has its own, and have the groups write the actual short story. This creates a good lesson on perception and communication in writing, and really sends a message to the students on how effective and necessary good description can be in their writing. This is cooperative learning at its best.

Although I did not mention oral presentations in the lesson, it is not uncommon for many of the groups to ask for the opportunity to show their ideas. If time permits, I always try to accommodate them.

FORMATTING YOUR STORY

Your group's assignment is to turn your picture into a format for the world's most creative short story. You are required to discuss your picture as a group and share your ideas. You will be creating the setting, the main character, and the plot of the story that your picture tells. You will not be writing this story, but instead focusing intently on the three elements mentioned. Imagination and creative writing will be required, and nothing less than brilliance will be accepted.

To provide the best possible format for your story, please follow these directions:

1. Write at least one page describing the setting of your story. Focus only on the setting and be as creative and visual as possible in your writing. (For example, "The grass rippled softly in the breeze, an ocean of green shimmering on the surface. The sky above was endless, clear and blue, with slight tinges of orange creeping just across the horizon.") The best way to determine everything about your setting is for you to imagine you are there, standing and looking around. What do you see, smell, and hear? What is the weather like? Think of as many details as possible and paint a picture with words that will put the reader at that place and time. Please be careful not to go into plot when describing—give only description, not what's going on.

2. Write at least one page describing the main character of your story. If your picture has no characters, you will need to invent one to go with your story. Focus on one main character for your story and write everything there is to know about your character. Leave the plot of the story out of your character description, and instead give your character a history on paper. Discuss among your group when your character was born (or created), where he or she was born, what his or her childhood was like, what his or her parents (or creator) were like, any events that shaped the way he or she is today, what he or she likes to eat, any music preferences, any odd habits, clothes he or she likes to wear, and anything else you want the reader to know. Be sure to include a good physical description of your character.

3. Write at least one page telling the plot of your story. Now is when you describe what your story is about. Please do not attempt to write the story, but instead give a summary of the sequence of events within the story. Also, with your plot summary, include an explanation of the conflict that will take place in the story and how it will be resolved. In your plot summary, be as creative and clever as possible. This is a good opportunity to show off your group's imagination. If your group finds it hard to summarize the plot and conflict with only a page of writing, you probably have some creative ideas that need more explanation—this is good.

From *Going Bohemian: How to Teach Writing Like You Mean It* (2nd edition) by Lawrence Baines & Anthony Kunkel. Copyright 2010 International Reading Association.

Crossing Edson's Bridge

Type of Activity
Individual

Approximate Time
Two or three 50-minute class periods

Objective
Students will gain creative writing skills, learn to analyze rhetorical techniques, and learn to identify imagery, metaphors, and figurative language within selected writing.

Summary
This lesson was designed for my 11th-grade Advanced Placement classes, but I have adapted it for regular 9th-grade classes as well. The results have produced some terrific student writing. I always try to allow time for students who want to read their stories aloud.

Materials
Copies of the "The Bridge" by Russell Edson handout (see p. 180)

Setup
None

Procedure
Step 1
Pass out the handout called "The Bridge" by Russell Edson (1996) and instruct students to read it silently to themselves.

Next, have them write a well-constructed essay, analyzing and discussing the imagery and metaphors used by Edson in his story. One class period should be plenty of time for this step to be accomplished.

Figure 22. A Student's Sequel to Russell Edson's "The Bridge"

Dear mother,

We have crossed the bone bridge. I was uncertain as to what to expect. Upon reaching the other end, we came upon a toll booth, of sorts. The guardian there was a serious, stone-faced man. He demanded to know our purpose in coming, or what we intended to do if we were permitted to pass. I had to admit that I didn't quite know. It was merely dependent on what we found across the way. Of course, being unable to tell this, as we might be denied passage, I made up a frivolous excuse, which, after some contemplation, the guardian grudgingly accepted. Descending the steps of the bridge, I looked out at the world around me. I had guessed right on one account; it was full of flesh, that is, people everywhere. It seemed a happy place after the bridge of bones. The ape shrieked behind me. He must see something I don't. I gave him my helmet to satisfy him for awhile, then continued on. I will write more later.

Step 2

Collect and redistribute all essays so that no student has his or her own writing.

Instruct students to analyze and score their given essays, paying close attention to how well they're constructed and how well the imagery and metaphors are discussed. Be sure to explain your expectations for this step, based on the level of the class.

Step 3

Briefly discuss Edson's story and the metaphors and imagery found within.

Then, ask students to write a sequel to Edson's story, beginning with the character having just "crossed the bridge." Students should attempt to model Edson's prose style and tone, striving to incorporate new imagery and metaphors. They should also pay close attention to the length of their sequel. Figure 22 illustrates the level of writing that might be produced in class.

Enrichment

This activity is an excellent setup for a unit on reading comprehension. Students not only become active readers but also critical writers. Having students write a second essay that analyzes the various stories that were produced in class changes the atmosphere from writing the traditional essay on selected reading to reading critically as a peer reviewer.

RESOURCE

Edson, R. (1977). "The bridge." In *The reason why the closet-man is never sad.* Middletown, CT: Wesleyan University Press.

"THE BRIDGE" BY RUSSELL EDSON

In his travels he comes to a bridge made entirely of bones. Before crossing he writes a letter to his mother: Dear mother, guess what? the ape accidentally bit off one of his hands while eating a banana. Just now I am at the foot of a bone bridge. I shall be crossing it shortly. I don't know if I shall find hills and valleys made of flesh on the other side, or simply constant night, villages of sleep. The ape is scolding me for not teaching him better. I am letting him wear my pith helmet for consolation. The bridge looks like one of those skeletal reconstructions of a huge dinosaur one sees in a museum. The ape is looking at the stump of his wrist and scolding me again. I offer him another banana and he gets very furious, as though I'd insulted him. Tomorrow we cross the bridge. I'll write to you from the other side if I can; if not, look for a sign...

From Russell Edson, "The Bridge," from *The Reason Why the Closet-Man Is Never Sad* © 1977 by Russell Edson and reprinted by permission of Wesleyan University Press.

Real Life:
Writing and Thinking

Regular opportunities to engage in activities that use different modes of discourse are...important to student growth. For example, the processes involved in responding to literature differ from those used in seeking information from texts and then presenting it to others. These modes must be taught, modeled, and practiced.

From "Language Arts" by James R. Squire, in G. Cawelti (Ed.),
Handbook of Research on Improving Student Achievement

Darrell, a student of yours who became a National Merit Scholar, had never been an eager fiction reader. "Why read stories that are made up?" he'd ask. "There's so much that I don't know about the *real* world." Although he was extremely bright, he preferred math, social studies, and science over English. To Darrell, fiction was not so much boring as irrelevant.

As an English teacher, you know that you are biased in favor of poetry and prose, and you confess that most of your students will not wind up as college English professors. But because scientists, journalists, and historians still communicate mostly with words, you attempt to work with your colleagues in other fields to bring an interdisciplinary approach to your classroom and theirs. Indeed, many of the best-known authors from the United States—John Steinbeck, Ernest Hemingway, Jack London, Michael Crichton, William Faulkner, Dorothy Parker, Flannery O'Connor, Toni Morrison, Joan Didion, James Baldwin, Jack Kerouac—have written nonfiction at one time or another. You like to give the future scientists in your classes an opportunity to create an elegant scientific report, the historians a chance to write pellucidly about significant historical figures, and the journalists an occasion to research and report with panache.

So you mix it up. You illuminate the diverse cultures in the United States, dig up startling statistics about American life, and provide abundant resources on the environment, sociological trends, and health. Then, you turn over the conversation to students by asking, "What does it all mean?" Their conclusions are not as important to you as the quality of their research, the logic of their thinking, and the eloquence of their arguments.

Teacher Spy

Type of Activity
Individual

Approximate Time
Two weeks for setup and two 50-minute class periods

Objective
Students will use skills of observation, a variety of descriptive writing techniques, and explicit detail to characterize a teacher at the school.

Summary
In many ways, having students write about teachers at their school is easier than asking students to write fictional stories out of the blue. First, the blank page does not impede students. Instead, they have pages of journal notes and a response sheet from which to draw.

Writing about a real teacher has the added advantage of being relevant in a visceral way to the students' lives. Not surprising, sometimes students use the character sketch to vent their negative feelings about a particular teacher or glorify a teacher they admire. Either way, it makes for lively writing.

Materials
Pen and paper

Setup
Two weeks before the class is to begin writing for this activity, ask students to begin tracking the habits of one particular teacher at school in a journal. In general, students seem to enjoy the "detective" aspect of this assignment. They should attempt to include observations of at least the following aspects of the teacher, although they may record their observations in any format they wish.

1. Choice of clothing

2. Facial features, including hairstyle and color

3. Favorite expressions or words, including a description of the teacher's voice

4. Typical interactions with students

5. Some likely aspirations or dreams of the teacher

6. Where the teacher might be in 10 years or what he or she might be doing then

7. Any other unique features or distinguishing characteristics

Procedure

Students should write out responses to these observations at the conclusion of their two-week journal assignment and before beginning the character sketch. Your initial check of these responses should focus on the explicitness of their recorded observations. For example, "He was a big guy" should not be allowed. Rather, a good physical description would be, "He was so tall that he had to duck his head as he stepped into the room after the tardy bell rang."

Students then write a character sketch from the details that they recorded about their chosen teachers, using their individual journals and their responses to the seven points mentioned earlier. Tell them that they should change the name of the teacher they describe. Most papers should have at least five paragraphs.

Once students think they have a finished draft, they should get at least three of their peers to critique it. The peers should

- Guess the identity of the teacher
- Give at least one additional detail about the teacher that the author did not note
- Give their impressions of the teacher, especially if they differ radically from the description they are reading
- Assess the degree of detail in the description and offer suggestions for improvement

After the peer edit, instruct the student-authors to revise at their discretion. In addition to the changes suggested by their peers, which

Figure 23. An Eighth-Grader's Teacher Spy Essay

She was a permanent feature of the school; she had been there for as long as anyone could remember. Every student knew, deep in his heart, that she would never retire; when she was 105, she would still croak from her hospital bed, "If you have permission to talk, stand up beside your seat."

She was a short, dumpling-like thing and looked perfectly harmless to the casual observer. But to those who appeared in class every morning, she was a holy terror.

She had grayish-white hair, short and permed. Her gold-rimmed glasses sat forever atop her head. Her large nose sat squarely amid fleshy, flabby jowls and a small pursed mouth that resembled a child's after tasting a lemon. She was always in style—last year's.

She invariably asked impossible questions that demanded impossible answers, while her steely brown eyes just dared the person asked to attempt a response.

Her voice was high, piercing, and nasal and caused the bursting of more than a few eardrums. Nevertheless, everyone slept. Eyelids began to droop until the Texan accent rose a pitch higher and brought sleepy heads wide awake.

Still, for all her faults, she is probably the one teacher I had who actually taught me about the beauty of mathematics, the joy of knowing that one correct answer exists somewhere out there in the universe. She taught me that the amount of suffering one goes through in solving a problem is usually proportional to the value of what has been learned. Kind of like life. It seemed such an ugly lesson at the time, but now I think I understand.

---

may or may not be heeded, special attention should be given to the final paragraph. Let them know that the final paragraph should draw from new data offered by peers, wrap up the essay, or give a new twist to the description. Figure 23 presents an eighth-grader's Teacher Spy essay.

Enrichment

An enlightening follow-up assignment is to have students write a character sketch about themselves from the teacher's perspective, using the same guidelines as they used for the character sketch of the teacher.

The Federal Government at Work

Type of Activity
Individual

Approximate Time
One or two 50-minute class periods

Objective
Students will discuss which social problems deserve immediate attention and financial support, and learn how the U.S. government spends its money.

Summary
The Federal Government at Work is a remarkable exercise. Having students use poker chips gives the decisions about expenditures a powerful, physical dimension, which helps anchor concepts for students who may have difficulty with abstract numbers. Indeed, after this exercise, students will long remember how the U.S. government spends its money.

Most adolescents have only a vague notion about their own values, let alone the values of their peers and of the American government (at least as expressed in dollar amounts). This little exercise in critical thinking helps bring into focus student beliefs, as well as the opinions of peers and the priorities of the federal government. It has the added benefit of providing current data on how the U.S. government is choosing to spend its money.

Materials
Pencil (with eraser) and paper, recent news stories about governmental spending or budgets, 50 poker chips (or pennies or whatever) per group, and one copy per group of the Our U.S. Federal Budget for 2008 handout (see p. 191) and the Actual U.S. Federal Budget for 2008 handout (see p. 192)

Setup

Be sure to hide the Actual U.S. Federal Budget for 2008 handouts until after the students have decided how funds should be spent, defended their views to the class, guessed at actual expenditures by the U.S. government, and announced their projections to the class.

Prepare a "hypothetical spending chart" on the chalkboard (or on a transparency on the overhead projector), so students can fill in how their groups wish to spend their money during their group presentations. This chart will look like the Our U.S. Federal Budget for 2008 handout, but there needs to be enough space for each group to write their answers next to each sector.

Procedure

Highlight any current events surrounding governmental spending or the federal deficit that you found in recent news stories.

Put students into groups of three or four and assign each group a number. The groups will present later on in numerical order. Ask them to divvy up the following roles: secretary (writes on the group's papers), lawyer (speaks/defends the group's decisions), public relations expert (writes on the chalkboard), and analyst (tries to find holes in the logic of the group's decisions and the decisions of the other groups). Groups need a place to spread out and will need an area to display their predictions. Placing several desks side by side or using a section of the floor will do.

Pass out one copy of the Our U.S. Federal Budget for 2008 handout and 50 poker chips to each group. Explain that each chip represents $50 billion for a total of $2.5 trillion.

Hand out 13 blank sheets of paper to each group. The group's secretary writes in large letters the name of the sectors on each sheet of paper (i.e., the secretary writes "Defense" on a piece of paper, "Social Security" on another sheet of paper, etc.).

Give students 15 to 20 minutes to decide as a group how they think the $2.5 trillion should be spent. To foster deliberations, discussion, and compromise, I recommend that group decisions be unanimous. However, if you see several individual students with the same kind of objections impeding decision making within the groups, you may recommend the formation of a spontaneous "radical group" of dissenters.

The secretary writes the final amount decided by the group for each sector on the Our U.S. Federal Budget for 2008 handout in the first blank column and includes the number of chips in parentheses as an accuracy check. So, if the paper labeled "Defense" on the group's paper has 5 poker chips sitting on it, the secretary would write "250 billion (5 chips)."

After each group has made a decision about how to apportion their $2.5 trillion, each group, led by the lawyer, reads its choices to the rest of the class and defends them, one by one. *Note:* While a group is initially presenting, the other groups must remain silent until the end of the presentation. While the lawyer presents the group's decision for each sector, the public relations expert writes the amount (and chips) for each sector on the chalkboard.

After a group has finished its presentation and rationale, the floor opens for debate, usually led by each group's analyst. Make sure to highlight significant differences and commonalities as you move from group to group. During debating time, encourage all students to defend the benefits and drawbacks of their groups' choices as well as the choices of other groups. Highlight analyses or criticisms that seem particularly astute (yea!) or especially incongruous (boo!). After all student presentations, you may want to rename each group, depending on how they chose to spend the money. For example, a group that spent massive amounts on energy, the environment, and education might be called "the greenies," whereas one that spent the most on the military might be called "the militants." Each secretary will write the new group name next to their number.

Keep the hypothetical spending chart in view as you proceed.

Next, each group should devote itself to predicting how the U.S. government actually spends its money. Students keep their same roles and follow the procedures already established: Chips are distributed by sector (all decisions must be unanimous), secretaries write the groups' guesstimates on their papers, lawyers present to the class, public relations experts write on the chalkboard, and group members defend their choices to the class and argue about the wisdom of their choices. You can mix up the order of group presentations by having them go in alphabetical order by group name for this round.

Finally, after discussion of the differences between how groups think the government should spend its money vs. the reality, pass out one copy of the Actual U.S. Federal Budget for 2008 handout to each group.

Have each group rearrange its chips to reflect actual U.S. expenditures, rounding numbers of chips to the nearest $50 billion. The secretary should write the actual amounts (and chips) on the group's original handout in the last blank column. You can also refer to the Office of Management and Budget's (n.d.) website for much more information on the U.S. federal budget.

Revealing federal expenditures should stimulate lively debate. Most of the time, students will be able to write an essay on the appropriateness of federal governmental expenditures with just this new piece of data. However, for students who struggle to put words to paper, responding to the following series of six questions, with each question representing one paragraph, will allow the paper to write itself:

1. What was the biggest surprise about the federal government's expenditures? Is the federal government making wise decisions with regard to how they are spending money? Why or why not?

2. What was the biggest disparity between actual U.S. spending in a sector and your group's decision about spending for that sector? Why was the difference between these two figures so great?

3. In what sector did your group's prediction about federal spending come closest to the real number? What accounts for the accuracy?

4. What were the wisest choices made by your group? Why are they good choices? Do they align with actual federal expenditures?

5. What were the least defensible choices made by your group? What makes those decisions weak?

6. How would the United States be different today if the government spent money as your group suggested?

Enrichment

A natural follow-up assignment would be "where tax dollars come from," which would examine the relative contributions of the wealthy, middle class, lower class, and poor to the tax base in the United States (see Moore, 2007, in the Resources section). The Tax Policy Center (2009) provides some nice summary tables, although you can get the entire annual budget through the Congressional Budget Office (2010) website as well.

RESOURCES

Congressional Budget Office (USA). (2010). *The budget and economic outlook: Fiscal years 2010 to 2020*. Retrieved February 23, 2010, from www.cbo.gov/ftpdocs/108xx/doc10871/Frontmatter.shtml

Moore, S. (2007, November/December). Guess who really pays the taxes. *The American*. Retrieved February 20, 2010, from www.american.com/archive/2007/november-december-magazine-contents/guess-who-really-pays-the-taxes

Office of Management and Budget, Executive Office of the President of the United States. (n.d.). *Budget of the United States Government: Fiscal year 2008*. Retrieved February 12, 2010, from www.whitehouse.gov/omb/rewrite/budget/fy2008/hist.html

Tax Policy Center, Urban Institute and Brookings Institution. (2009). *The numbers: What are the federal government's sources of revenue?* Retrieved February 23, 2010, from www.taxpolicycenter.org/briefing-book/background/numbers/revenue.cfm

OUR U.S. FEDERAL BUDGET FOR 2008

Imagine that your group has to decide on the U.S. federal budget. You have 50 chips, and each chip is worth $50 billion. So, you are deciding on how to spend $2.5 trillion! First, decide how much you would give to the following sectors. All decisions must be unanimous. On a separate blank sheet, make labels for each sector below and stack the corresponding number of chips on each label. Later, your group will guess how much was actually given in the 2008 federal budget.

Group number (round 1): Group name (round 2): Sector	Group allotment in billions (and in chips)	Group guess at the actual allotment in billions (and in chips)	Actual U.S. federal budget in billions (and in chips)
Social Security (income for people over age 65)			
Defense (includes wars in Iraq and Afghanistan)			
Medicare (health care for people over age 65)			
Medicaid (health insurance for the poor—might be under or over age 65)			
Education (K–12 public education, higher education, job training, and vocational training)			
Transportation (interstate roads, and support for airports and trains)			
Veteran's benefits (disability compensation, pensions, education, home loans, life insurance, vocational rehabilitation, survivors' benefits, medical benefits, and burial benefits)			
Administration of justice (including Antitrust, Civil Disturbances, Civil Rights, Crime, Environment and Natural Resources, Justice, National Security, and Tax Evasion)			
Environmental Protection Agency (natural resources and the environment)			
Foreign affairs (protecting U.S. citizens living or traveling abroad, assisting U.S. businesses in the international marketplace, official visits overseas and at home, and other diplomatic efforts)			
Agriculture (distribution of food, aid to farmers, crops, and nutrition)			
Energy (energy policy and nuclear safety, nuclear reactor production for the U.S. Navy, energy conservation, energy-related research, radioactive waste disposal, and domestic energy production)			
Welfare and unemployment (government payments to the poor)			

ACTUAL U.S. FEDERAL BUDGET FOR 2008

For chip allocation, numbers have been rounded, in most cases, to the nearest $50 billion.

Sector	Actual federal budget in billions (and in chips)
Social Security (income for people over age 65)	644 (13)
Defense (includes wars in Iraq and Afghanistan)	660 (13)
Medicare (health care for people over age 65)	408 (8)
Medicaid (health insurance for the poor—might be under or over age 65)	224 (4)
Education (K–12 public education, higher education, job training, and vocational training)	45 (1)
Transportation (interstate roads, and support for airports and trains)	11 (0)
Veteran's benefits (disability compensation, pensions, education, home loans, life insurance, vocational rehabilitation, survivors' benefits, medical benefits, and burial benefits)	45 (1)
Administration of justice (including Antitrust, Civil Disturbances, Civil Rights, Crime, Environment and Natural Resources, Justice, National Security, and Tax Evasion)	20 (1)
Environmental Protection Agency (natural resources and the environment)	7 (0)
Foreign affairs (protecting U.S. citizens living or traveling abroad, assisting U.S. businesses in the international marketplace, official visits overseas and at home, and other diplomatic efforts)	1 (0)
Agriculture (distribution of food, aid to farmers, crops, and nutrition)	20 (1)
Energy (energy policy and nuclear safety, nuclear reactor production for the U.S. Navy, energy conservation, energy-related research, radioactive waste disposal, and domestic energy production)	25 (1)
Welfare and unemployment (government payments to the poor)	360 (7)

Data from *Budget of the United States Government: Fiscal Year 2008*, Office of Management and Budget, Executive Office of the President of the United States, n.d., retrieved February 12, 2010, from www.whitehouse.gov/omb/rewrite/budget/fy2008/hist.html.

Research Brochure

Type of Activity
Group

Approximate Time
One or two 50-minute class periods

Objective
Students will research a topic, write notes, take photos, and compile everything into an informational brochure.

Summary
Shooting digital photographs and writing text that will be encapsulated, arranged, and presented to peers within a short time frame has a way of intensifying student interest and effort. The process also follows what most investigative reporters, nonfiction book authors, and scholars do as a matter of course. Of course, engagement and motivation are crucial to the success of any academic enterprise, perhaps most of all for struggling students and those whose primary language is not English.

Research Brochure adds urgency and relevance to the task of discovering information and presenting research. A nice bonus is that the brochures transport well; students can put brochures in their back pockets and pull them out later to show to friends and family.

Materials
Digital cameras, research materials (books, articles, and websites), and a computer with publishing software, such as Microsoft Publisher or any other free publishing software available online

Setup
Choose several research topics that can be completed within a few hours and have them ready for class. In the past, I used these topics successfully:

art in public places, the mathematics of leaves, most-nutritious meals at McDonald's, cliques, furniture, sports, and the aesthetics of school buildings.

Procedure

Have students select from among several topics. Tell them they must cite at least two articles and passages from at least one book. I recommend requiring a "worksheet" containing at least five direct citations from texts replete with bibliographic information, a summary of findings, and images of all contributors.

Then, students meet to discuss their findings, synthesize results, and highlight the most significant or interesting information.

Students use digital cameras to shoot at least five images related to the topic. Students also take a portrait (head shot) of each member of the group.

Set a date and time for completed presentations and discuss the rubric for assessment. I usually use a straightforward evaluation tool, such as the following criteria:

- Quality of information (accuracy and relevance) = 20%.
- Quality of written expression (eloquence and conciseness) = 20%.
- Five citations from at least three different sources of information (minimum two articles and one book) = 20%.
- Quality of images (at least five of their chosen topic and one of each group member) = 20%.
- Aesthetics and arrangement of text and photos = 20%.

A portion of the grade is earmarked for aesthetically pleasing presentation and graphic design. The student work provided in Figures 24, 25, and 26 relate to the topic "The Mathematics of Leaves," in which part of the students' task was to calculate the surface area of leaves that they find on school grounds. Figure 24 shows the students' math calculations, Figure 25 is the final brochure, and Figure 26 is the students' listing of citations.

Figure 24. A Student Group's Mathematical Work Pages for Researching "The Mathematics of Leaves"

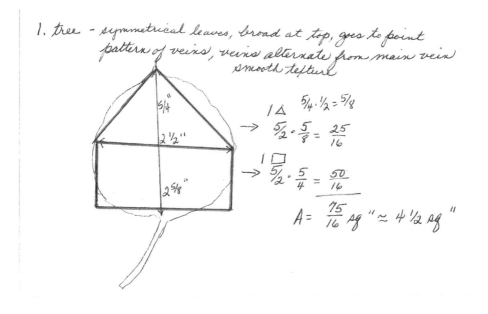

1. tree – symmetrical leaves, broad at top, goes to point
   pattern of veins, veins alternate from main vein
   smooth texture

$5/4''$

$2\frac{1}{2}''$

$2\frac{5}{8}''$

$1\,\triangle$ $\frac{5}{4} \cdot \frac{1}{2} = \frac{5}{8}$

$\rightarrow$ $\frac{5}{2} \cdot \frac{5}{8} = \frac{25}{16}$

$1\,\square$

$\rightarrow$ $\frac{5}{2} \cdot \frac{5}{4} = \frac{50}{16}$

$A = \frac{75}{16}$ sq $'' \approx 4\frac{1}{2}$ sq $''$

2. bush – symmetrical leaves, resemble maple leaf, rough texture

$\frac{3}{2}''$

$\frac{3}{2}''$

$2\frac{5}{8}$

$3\frac{3}{4}''$

$1\,\triangle$ $\frac{3}{4} \cdot \frac{3}{2} = \frac{9}{8} = \frac{72}{64}$

$1\,\square$ $\frac{25}{8} \cdot \frac{17}{8} = \frac{425}{64}$

$A = \frac{497}{64} \approx 7\frac{3}{4}$ sq in.

(continued)

3. perennial flower - small, fan-shaped, rough texture, rippled edges

$1\triangle \frac{3}{8} \cdot \frac{9}{8} = \frac{27}{64}$

$1\square \frac{1}{4} \cdot \frac{9}{8} = \frac{9}{32} + \frac{27}{64} = \frac{45}{64}$ sq. in. $\approx \frac{3}{4}$ sq "

4. sedum - rubbery texture, succulent, more dense

$\frac{1}{2} \cdot \frac{1}{4} = \frac{1}{8}$

$\left(\frac{1}{2} \cdot \frac{1}{2}\right) = \frac{1}{4}$

$A = \frac{3}{8}$ sq "

5. tree - green to rust-colored, smooth texture

$\triangle \frac{7}{8} \cdot \frac{11}{8} = \frac{77}{64}$

fat $\triangle \frac{7}{8} \cdot \frac{11}{8} = \frac{88}{64}$

$A = \frac{165}{64} \approx 2\frac{1}{2}$ sq "

6. grass - grainy texture
dark green to light green
from inside to outside

$\square \quad A = 12 \cdot \frac{1}{2} = 6$ sq. in

7. plant - burgundy leaf

$\triangle \frac{9}{8} \cdot \frac{3}{4} = \frac{21}{32}$

$\square \frac{7}{8} \cdot \frac{3}{2} = \frac{42}{32}$

$A = \frac{69}{32}$ sq "

$\approx 2\frac{1}{6}$ sq "

Figure 25. A Student Group's Research Brochure for "The Mathematics of Leaves"

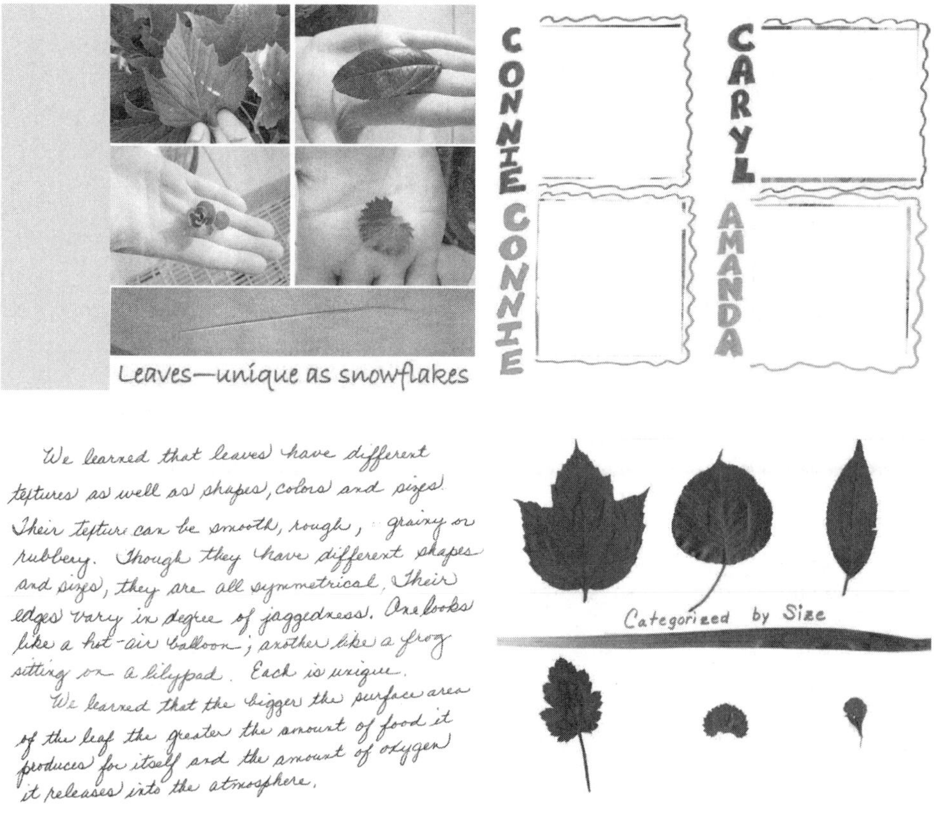
Leaves—unique as snowflakes
CONNIE
CARYL
CONNIE
AMANDA
We learned that leaves have different textures as well as shapes, colors and sizes. Their texture can be smooth, rough, grainy or rubbery. Though they have different shapes and sizes, they are all symmetrical. Their edges vary in degree of jaggedness. One looks like a hot-air balloon; another like a frog sitting on a lilypad. Each is unique.
We learned that the bigger the surface area of the leaf the greater the amount of food it produces for itself and the amount of oxygen it releases into the atmosphere.
Categorized by Size

Enrichment

Consider assigning students different aspects of a particular problem. For example, one group of students could focus on the potential benefits of biotechnology, such as eradicating cancer, while another group could focus on the potential dangers of biotechnology, such as the creation of new, synthetic, destructive life forms.

Figure 26. A Student Group's Citations for "The Mathematics of Leaves"

1. Excerpt from the poem "Woods" by Wendell Berry:

   I part the out thrusting branches
   and come in beneath
   the blessed and the blessing trees.
   Though I am silent
   there is singing around me.

2. Excerpt from the poem "Lord, the air smells good..." by Rumi:

   The trees in their prayer, the birds in praise,
   the first blue violets kneeling.
   Whatever came from Being is caught up in being, drunkenly
   forgetting the way back.

3. From the website Wikiquote (en.wikiquote.org/wiki/Nature):

   "The tree which moves some to tears of joy is in the eyes of others only a green thing that stands in the way. Some see nature all ridicule and deformity...and some scarce see nature at all. But to the eyes of the man of imagination, nature is imagination itself." —William Blake (1757–1827)

4. Three quotes from *Tree*, edited by J. Lacock, 2005, New York: Dorling Kindersley:

   "The earliest 'plants' were so small that it would have taken dozens of them to cover a pinhead." (p. 6)
   "Perhaps because of the size and long life of trees, many religions have regarded them as sacred symbols, and certain individual trees have been worshiped as gods." (p. 6)
   "Five thousand years ago, before the spread of agriculture, huge areas of Europe and eastern North America were cloaked in broadleaved forest. Since then much of the forest has been cleared to make way for people." (p. 8)

5. Excerpt from the poem "Birches" by Robert Frost:

   I'd like to go by climbing a birch tree
   And climb black branches up a snow-white trunk
   Toward heaven, till the tree could bear no more,
   But dipped its top and set me down again.

6. From *A Tree Is Growing*, by A. Dorros, 1997, New York: Scholastic, p. 3:

   "Bristlecone pines are the oldest known living trees on earth. Some have been growing for five thousand years—since before the pyramids in Egypt were built."

7. From *A Natural History of Western Trees*, by D.C. Peattie, 1991). Boston: Houghton Mifflin, p. 12:

   "The Coast Redwood, the ever-living Sequoia, sempervirens, is the tallest tree in the world.... A Redwood has a normal life expectancy of 1000 to 1500 years."

Survivor!

Type of Activity
Individual

Approximate Time
One 50-minute class period

Objective
Students will learn about survival techniques advocated by a former member of the U.S. Army Special Forces and compare these techniques with the actions of fictional and real characters in survival situations.

Summary
I used to begin the study of Jack London's (1983) "To Build a Fire" with a winter survival test. Students rated the gear they would need to survive in Alaska during the winter and provided a rationale for their choices. Then, I handed out the collected wisdom of experts from sources such as *Outside* magazine and self-proclaimed survivalists and asked students to compare their selections against the experts'. Although the opinions of students and experts rarely aligned, students absolutely loved the activity.

However, what bothered me about my winter survival exercise was that some of the advice from my expert sources seemed vague and, at times, contradictory. I feel better about the veracity of suggestions offered by Myke Hawke, a Green Beret and former captain in the U.S. Army Special Forces, because he actually lived through a plethora of survival situations and wrote about them. His knowledge is so revered that he teaches survival skills to members of elite fighting forces for the U.S. military.

Part of the lure of Survivor! is the incredible gap that exists between the daily reality of contemporary student life and the uncomfortable, stark, life-and-death realities of surviving in the wild. Today, students eat burgers from McDonald's, sleep in comfortable beds in safe homes, and download whatever their hearts desire to their iPhones. The prospect of being stripped of all electronics and thrown into a non-mall setting where insects, beasts, hunger, thirst, and weather threaten their very existence often energizes even the most apathetic students. In case students ask (and they will), most humans can live only three days without water and three weeks without food, on average.

Materials

Use the book *Hawke's Green Beret Survival Manual* by Myke Hawke (2009), an expert on survival skills, and excerpts from books such as *Hatchet* by Gary Paulsen (2006), *Into Thin Air* by Jon Krakauer (2009), *Robinson Crusoe* by Daniel Defoe (2009; the section when Crusoe is shipwrecked on the Island of Despair), *The Call of the Wild* by Jack London (2000), or any other books or stories having to do with survival in a wilderness area. Another reliable source for survival information is the *U.S. Army Survival Manual* (U.S. Department of the Army, 2009), although Hawke frequently elucidates this manual's shortcomings.

You'll also need copies of the Survival Choices: Character Actions and Survival Choices: Expert Suggestions handouts (see pp. 203 and 204).

I bring in props such as rope, grass, twigs, a canteen, a plastic knife, a blanket, and any other objects that might be used in a quest for survival. Use a short clip (5–10 minutes) from any film about survival, such as the film versions of *Hatchet* or *Robinson Crusoe*, or a clip from a recent episode of the reality television show *Survivor*. The focus should be the first day or two in the wilderness, when the probabilities for death or life are established.

Setup

If available, show students a brief film clip of someone finding himself or herself lost in the wilderness that includes the individual's initial actions, hesitancy, and difficulties. For example, the film version of *Hatchet* was shot on location where Paulsen set the story—in the Canadian wilderness during the summer. Show the clip where the helicopter crashes and Brian bails out and makes it to shore. As an alternative, have students read a story of someone surviving in the wild.

Note that survival skills for severe, arctic-type cold (such as on a glacier where nothing grows) or extreme, Sahara desert–type situations may differ from survival skills in forested or mountainous areas. However, other than in extreme conditions of hot and cold, survival skills for forests and mountains are applicable to a wide variety of conditions and situations, including urban survival. Thus, this exercise would also be suitable for the study of apocalyptic books such as Meg Rosoff's (2004) *How I Live Now*, Richard Matheson's (2007) *I Am Legend*, William Golding's (1959) *Lord of the Flies*, Cormac McCarthy's (2009) *The Road*, or Nevil Shute's (2010) *The Beach*.

Procedure

After students view the film clip or read the story of someone attempting to survive in a wilderness environment, ask them to consider the actions of the individual and assess the wisdom of his or her actions. Students write out responses to the following questions:

- What did he or she do?
- What mistakes were made?
- What should have been done first?
- What was neglected?
- What would have been the best course of action?

Then, have students also fill out the Survival Choices: Character Actions handout for each character.

If the story involves more than one survivor, ask students to rate the survivors in the story based on their thoughts and actions. Who was the smartest? Who had the worst response? Why?

Next, students read excerpts from Hawke's *Green Beret Survival Manual* or the Survival Choices: Expert Suggestions handout. They then write a response to Hawke's advice, from the book or the handout, comparing their evaluations and comments against his advice.

Finally, students read a passage from a different story or film and repeat the process, describing the survivor's mistakes and smart moves and completing a Survival Choices: Character Actions handout for each character.

Then, students pool the characters from both stories and rank each character according to how they think Hawke would rate them along with a rationale for their ratings.

Enrichment

Once students have analyzed the survival responses of fictional and real characters in the wild, give them the opportunity to write their own adventure. Place students in pairs and give each pair a survival situation printed on an index card. A card might include the following:

> Your name is Andy Anderson and you are a policeman in New Orleans. The date is August 28, 2005, the day before Hurricane Katrina hits, and the time is midnight. You have been assigned by Police Captain LeTour to watch the Ninth Ward area of the city. Write about what happens on your job on this night, the effects of the hurricane, how you survive, and how (and if) you help others survive.

If you do not feel like writing out a set of index cards for the entire class, you can always resort to Joshua Piven's (2001) *The Worst-Case Scenario Survival Handbook: Travel,* which lists every possible travel disaster along with suggestions for coping with them.

RESOURCES

Defoe, D. (2009). *Robinson Crusoe.* New York: Oxford University Press.

Golding, W. (1959). *Lord of the flies.* New York: Perigee.

Hawke, M. (2009). *Hawke's Green Beret survival manual.* Philadelphia: Running Press.

Krakauer, J. (2009). *Into thin air: A personal account of the Mount Everest disaster.* New York: Anchor.

London, J. (1983). "To build a fire." In *The best short stories of Jack London* (pp. 13–27). New York: Ballantine.

London, J. (2000). *The call of the wild.* New York: Scholastic.

Matheson, R. (2007). *I am legend.* New York: Tor.

McCarthy, C. (2009). *The road.* New York: Vintage.

Paulsen, G. (2006). *Hatchet.* New York: Aladdin.

Piven, J. (2001). *The worst-case scenario survival handbook: Travel.* San Francisco: Chronicle.

Rosoff, M. (2004). *How I live now.* New York: Wendy Lamb.

Shute, N. (2010). *On the beach.* New York: Vintage.

U.S. Department of the Army. (2009). *The U.S. Army survival manual: Department of the Army field manual 21-76.* Berkeley, CA: Ulysses.

SURVIVAL CHOICES: CHARACTER ACTIONS

The example in column 1 below refers to Brian in Gary Paulsen's book *Hatchet*. Fill in column 2 (and column 3 if applicable) for your character(s).

Individual	1. Brian	2. _____	3. _____
Location	Canadian wilderness		
Main Tools	Hatchet		
Shelter	Cave, lean-to shelter		
Water	Lake		
Food	Wild cherries		
Smart Moves	Swam to safety, eventually went back to helicopter for supplies		
Mistakes	Initially dumb about food, water, and shelter		

From *Going Bohemian: How to Teach Writing Like You Mean It* (2nd edition) by Lawrence Baines & Anthony Kunkel. Copyright 2010 International Reading Association.

SURVIVAL CHOICES: EXPERT SUGGESTIONS

Individual	Green Beret
Location	Most wilderness areas
Main Tools	The knife and the stick are the only indispensable tools. The stick should be a foot taller than you and have a sharp point at one end. Your hand should wrap three fourths of the way around it. Use all equipment you can find.
Shelter	"The first rule in all cases, really, is to get off the ground. I always look to the trees for shelter first when I need shelter fast. It gets me off the ground and keeps me safe from most things—flash floods, mean beasties, and bad bugs...find two good branches—one to sit on, straddle, or otherwise hold you up, with another one close enough to wedge yourself in so you won't fall out. And then let the rest of your body lean against the base of the tree." (p. 43)
Water	Look for water at the lowest point. Water should be boiled. Failing that, use 5 drops of 10% bleach for every gallon of water, shake vigorously, and let sit for 30 minutes. Failing boiling or bleaching, get water by using your clothes to soak up the morning dew and squeeze the water absorbed by your clothes into your mouth. Follow birds, animals, and insects (but not reptiles) to water sources.
Food	Eat animals and insects instead of plants. "Almost everything out there moving around is edible in one way or another, whereas it's the other way around for plants—most plants are not edible for humans." (p. 184)
Smart Moves	Eat only safe berries: 90% of purple, blue, or black berries are okay; 50% of red berries are okay, but the other 50% could kill you; and 90% of all other berries are bad for you.
Mistakes	Good rules to follow: Get out of harm's way; provide first aid to yourself, then help others; be conscious of shelter, water, fire, and food; and decide to stay where you are or to leave the area to find help. If in doubt, stay where you are.

Adapted from *Hawke's Green Beret Survival Manual*, by M. Hawke, 2009, Philadelphia: Running Press.

Turning Point

Type of Activity
Individual and group

Approximate Time
One or two 50-minute class periods

Objective
Students will learn to associate turning points in literary fiction with turning points in nonfiction, music, and real life.

Summary
One of the problems with teaching literature in the 21st century is that many students do not see literature as relevant to their lives. By easing students into a literary experience through oral storytelling (the summary of the work at the beginning of the lesson) and intrigue (not revealing the end of the story), then following up with music and a real-life vignette, the hope is that students will begin to understand the possibilities of literature as a "lived through" experience.

Materials
Excerpts from great works of literature that revolve around a turning point: Most short stories and novels contain plot points where the protagonist makes a key decision. For example, Sethe decides to kill her children rather than have them be recaptured and sentenced to a life of slavery in Toni Morrison's *Beloved*, Sidney Carton decides to substitute himself for Charles Darnay so that Darnay's life will be spared at the guillotine in Charles Dickens's *A Tale of Two Cities*, and Hamlet decides he must act to avenge his father's death in William Shakespeare's play.

For the nonfiction piece, I recommend using an excerpt from Chapter 1 of Oliver Sacks's (2008) *Musicophilia* and the piano music "Lightning Sonata" by Tony Cicoria (2008, tracks 1–3). If you do not have time to locate and copy pages from *Musicophilia,* you may want to have copies of the down and dirty version in the Musicophilia handout (see p. 209).

Setup

Have the literary selections and music ready to go.

Procedure

Summarize the main plot and characters of a favorite literary work so that students will understand the gist of a story. Then, read an excerpt near the climax when one of the main characters makes an important decision. Stop reading before revealing the result of the decision. Ask students what they think will happen and write some possibilities on the chalkboard.

Read enough of the rest of the story for students to learn what the results of the decision were. Ask the students what other decisions the character could have made that would have resulted in a different outcome. Also, ask them to describe both the decision (cause) and the possible outcome (effect).

Play "Lightning Sonata" by Tony Cicoria. Do not reveal either the title of the work or the composer. Ask students to write a response to the music. In their response, students should try to answer the following four prompts:

1. Describe the music.

2. What is the composer writing about?

3. Describe the composer. What kind of person is he or she?

4. Why did he or she write this music?

Have students read their responses aloud and write on the chalkboard particularly descriptive or interesting comments.

Place students in groups of three or four. If you choose not to use your own excerpts from *Musicophilia,* pass out the Musicophilia handout and have students read it aloud in small groups. Have students compare their impressions of the music and composer against Cicoria's real-life story within their groups, then discuss the comparisons as a class.

Figure 27. 11th and 12th Graders' Turning Point Responses

1. The music moves from pretty, high notes to loud, bass chords. It sounds like someone is wrestling with himself, trying to figure out what to do next. There is some pressure and an urgency to the decision. Some of the low notes sound like explosions, and some of the high notes sound like wind chimes. It seems like there should be a cymbal, but there is only a piano playing. The music gets more and more restless. There is no satisfaction, no finish to the story.
2. The composer is probably trying to decide on something. On one side is violence and a storm; on the other side is rest and peace.
3. The composer is a confused guy. He does not know if he should rage and scream or kick back and accept life as it is.
4. He wrote the music, not to figure out anything, but to just describe what he was going through. There is all this emotion that needs to get out and music is his only way out.

Last year I thought I was in love. For almost a year, I was dating a guy who was in the army, and I thought he was going to ask me to marry him. But, he didn't. Instead, he got called up and went to Iraq. He wrote me once while he was over there, and I wrote him back. Then, I wrote him back again. But, no answer. Then, he kind of disappeared. I don't think he died or anything. I think he just decided that he didn't want me for his girlfriend any more.

If we would have gotten married, I probably would not have finished high school. I might be living in a town where there's a military base. I could have a kid and be living in a house somewhere.

Have students ponder their own lives and write about a turning point they experienced. Since these writings will be read by their peers, students should not share any turning points that they want to keep private. Figure 27 shows some of the answers that a class of 11th and 12th graders provided for the four questions, followed by a personal Turning Point piece.

After completing the assignment, have students exchange and read about the turning points of each student in their groups. After all group members have read all the papers, students draw a horizontal line on their papers beneath their writings. Below the horizontal line, they are to write about what would have happened differently in their lives had they made a different decision.

Enrichment

A fun follow-up activity that works as a fascinating study in human behavior is to have students write out a fact that "no one knows about me" or "people would be surprised to learn about me." Again, students should not reveal anything too incriminating, because responses will be read aloud.

Assign each student a secret number, which they will write at the top of the page. They should not write their name or give any hint as to authorship on their paper. To avoid detection through handwriting or color of ink or paper, papers should be printed off a computer or written in black ink on uniform pieces of paper. Take up the papers, shuffle them, and hand out one paper to every student in class.

Hand out a sheet of paper with the names of everyone in class on it as well. Give each student a minute to read the paper and make a guess as to its authorship, noting the number of the paper next to the name of the student they think wrote it. Then, have students pass the papers to the next person until they have read everyone's papers and made their guesses.

Last, take up the paragraphs and read them aloud. Note for whom most of the class voted and, finally, announce the true author. Students keep track of the correct number of guesses. The students with the most correct answers are usually those who are the most astute judges of human character.

RESOURCES
Cicoria, T. (2008). *Notes from an "accidental" pianist and composer* [CD]. United States: Dr. Tony Cicoria. ASIN: B001JTU4NY.
Sacks, O. (2008). *Musicophilia: Tales of music and the brain* (Rev. ed.). New York: Vintage.

MUSICOPHILIA: TONY CICORIA

Tony Cicoria, a forty-two-year-old orthopedic surgeon, was making a phone call to his mother when he was struck in the face by lightning. He thought he was dead immediately following the event but sustained no serious injuries and went back to work a few weeks later. But then, quite unexpectedly, he experienced an intense craving to listen to piano music—something he had never felt before. He started listening to piano music all the time, couldn't get enough of it. Then, a little later, he started hearing piano music in his head, insistently and powerfully; he felt the need to write it down, though he had no training in musical notation. Soon he was teaching himself to play the piano, playing the tunes that came to him unbidden at all moments. He played the piano at every opportunity, driving his wife to distraction. He had a bad case of sudden-onset musicophilia, somehow triggered by the brain alterations wrought by the lightning. He had become, in effect, a completely new person, evidently because of having had his brain electrically rewired.

Excerpted from "The Musical Mystery," by C. McGinn, March 6, 2008, *The New York Review of Books, 55*(3), para. 5, retrieved December 31, 2009, from www.nybooks.com/articles/21059.

Same Facts, Different Audience

Type of Activity
Group (could be adapted easily for individual work)

Approximate Time
Three 50-minute class periods

Objective
Students will consider how presentation of content, style, voice, and tone affect audience, medium, and purpose.

Summary
Not only do students gain knowledge about current issues of the world, but also they learn how audience, purpose, and medium help determine content, tone, style, and voice.

Materials
Pen and paper, and copies of the Youth and Violence in America Fact Sheet handout (see pp. 212–213), the Same Facts, Different Audience handout (see p. 214), and related articles (or television news clips)

For the purposes of this lesson description, violence at school will serve as the topic. If you prefer not to use the Youth and Violence in America Fact Sheet handout, you can create your own fact sheet for the students on any topic you wish, such as school policy, international affairs, environmental issues, or any current hot topic.

Setup
Discuss a recent incident of violence, either on your campus or at a school nearby. (Again, for the purposes of this lesson description, the topic of discussion is school violence.)

Procedure

Hand out printed articles about violence in schools or show related video clips from television news reports. Ask students to predict the prevalence of violence at schools nationally and write student predictions on the chalkboard, overhead, or computer.

Hand out the Youth and Violence in America Fact Sheet (or the one you created) and discuss it as a class. Explain why the trends and issues represented by the data are important.

Divide the class into groups of three and distribute the Same Facts, Different Audience handout. Instruct students to choose three projects on which they would like to work, one from each category: (1) writing texts for a receptive adolescent and adult audience, (2) writing for elementary-age children in a predominantly visual medium, and (3) writing texts for a resistant audience. Each group member should serve as the person responsible for completion of one of the three tasks. Thus, although students work together on all three projects, each assignment will have a main author.

Once students finish their projects (usually by the third day), they should present their results to the rest of the class. As each group makes its presentation, the rest of the class should assess the degree to which each project achieved its desired goal.

After all groups have presented, have students analyze the different kinds of appeals that were used within each category. For example, what kinds of techniques were used in attempting to persuade a resistant audience?

Enrichment

You may request that students do projects individually. You also might have a variety of fact sheets available so that students may choose among a variety of topics.

RESOURCES

American Bar Association. (2009). *Special committee on gun violence*. Retrieved March 29, 2010, from www.abanet.org/dch/committee.cfm?com=CC108570

Institute of Education Sciences, National Center for Education Statistics, U.S. Department of Education. (2009). *Indicators of school crime and safety: 2009* (NCES 2010-012). Washington, DC: Author.

YOUTH AND VIOLENCE IN AMERICA
FACT SHEET[a]

Violent deaths[b]:

- From July 1, 2007, through June 30, 2008, there were 21 homicides and 5 suicides of school-age youth (ages 5–18) at school, or about 1 homicide or suicide of a school-age youth at school per 2.1 million students enrolled during the 2007–2008 school year.

Nonfatal student and teacher victimization[b]:

- Although there was an overall decline in the victimization rates for students ages 12–18 at school between 1992 and 2007, there was no measurable difference in the rate of crime at school between 2004 and 2007. Between 1992 and 2007, the rate of crime for students away from school declined.

- The rates for theft and violent crime were higher at school than away from school. Students were victims of 31 thefts per 1,000 students at school, compared to 21 thefts per 1,000 students away from school. At school, there were 26 violent crimes per 1,000 students, compared to 20 violent crimes per 1,000 students away from school.

- Of students ages 12–18, 4% reported being victimized at school during the previous 6 months: 3% reported theft and 3% reported violent victimization. Less than 0.5% of students reported serious violent victimization.

- Of male students in grades 9–12, 10% reported being threatened or injured with a weapon on school property in the past year.

- A greater percentage of teachers in city schools (10%) reported being threatened with injury than teachers in town schools (7%) and suburban or rural schools (6% each).

School environment[b]:

- One or more incidents of crime took place at 85% of public schools, amounting to an estimated 2 million crimes. This figure translates to a rate of 43 crimes per 1,000 public school students enrolled in 2007–2008.

- At least 1 violent incident was reported to police at 38% of public schools.

- Of students ages 12–18, 23% reported that there were gangs at their schools.

- Of all students in grades 9–12, 22% reported that someone had offered, sold, or given them an illegal drug on school property in the past 12 months.

- Of students ages 12–18, 32% reported having been bullied at school during the school year.

- Just over one third (34%) of teachers agreed or strongly agreed that student misbehavior interfered with their teaching.

(continued)

From *Going Bohemian: How to Teach Writing Like You Mean It* (2nd edition) by Lawrence Baines & Anthony Kunkel. Copyright 2010 International Reading Association.

YOUTH AND VIOLENCE IN AMERICA
FACT SHEET[a] (continued)

Fights, weapons, and illegal substances[b]:

- 12% of students said they had been in a fight on school property during the preceding 12 months.

- 6% of students reported they had carried a weapon on school property during the previous 30 days.

Gun violence:

- In 2003, 2,827 children and teens died as a result of gun violence—more than the number of U.S. fighting men and women killed in hostile action in Iraq from 2003 to April 2006.[c]

- From 1985 through the early 1990s, the use of handguns in homicides committed by youth under the age of 18 increased nearly 4 times and handgun homicides by those ages 18–24 doubled. (From "Youth, Guns, and Violent Crime," by A. Blumstein, 2002, *The Future of Children, 12*(2), 39–54.)[d]

- Thirty-four percent of children in the United States (representing more than 22 million children in 11 million homes) live in homes with at least one firearm. In 69 percent of homes with firearms and children, more than one firearm is present.[e]

- The rate of death from firearms in the United States is 8 times higher than that in most industrial countries. (From "Preventing Firearm Injuries," by A.L. Kellermann & J.F. Waeckerle, 1998, *Annals of Emergency Medicine, 32*(1), 77–79.)[d]

- The overall firearm-related death rate among U.S. children younger than 15 years of age is nearly 12 times higher than among children in most other industrialized countries. (From "Rates of Homicide, Suicide, and Firearm-Related Death Among Children— 26 Industrialized Countries," by Centers for Disease Control and Prevention, 1997, *Morbidity and Mortality Weekly Report, 46*(5), 101–105.)[d]

- The United States has the highest rate of youth homicides and suicides among the 26 wealthiest nations. (From "Childhood Homicide, Suicide, and Firearm Deaths: An International Comparison," by E.G. Krug, L.L. Dahlberg, & K.E. Powell, 1996, *World Health Statistics Quarterly, 49*(3/4), 230–235.)[d]

[a]Unless otherwise specified, data relate to the 2007–2008 school year. [b]Data from *Indicators of School Crime and Safety: 2009* (NCES 2010-012), by the Institute of Education Sciences, National Center for Education Statistics, U.S. Department of Education, 2009, Washington, DC: Author. [c]Data from *CDF Gun Report: 2,827 Child, Teen Deaths by Firearms in One Year Exceed Total U.S. Combat Fatalities During Three Years in Iraq*, by Children's Defense Fund, 2006, retrieved March 30, 2010, from www.commondreams.org/news2006/0613-01.htm. [d]Data from *Special Committee on Gun Violence*, by the American Bar Association, 2009, retrieved March 29, 2010, from www.abanet.org/dch/committee.cfm?com=CC108570. [e]Data from *Guns in the Family: Firearm Storage Patterns in U.S. Homes With Children*, by Rand Corporation, 2001, retrieved March 30, 2010, from www.rand.org/pubs/research_briefs/RB4535/index1.html.

SAME FACTS, DIFFERENT AUDIENCE

<u>Please select one topic from each of these three groups:</u>

1. Writing texts for a receptive adolescent and adult audience:

   a. Create a survey concerning student fears and perceptions of violence at your school. Contrast the results with national data.

   b. Write a letter to the editor of a local newspaper, a news feature story, or a column for the student newspaper commenting on the role of violence in contemporary life.

   c. Write a fictional short story that should persuade a peer to take action to halt the proliferation of violence in schools.

2. Writing for elementary-age children in a predominantly visual medium:

   a. Create a television commercial suitable for airing on Saturday morning that alerts young children to the danger of guns.

   b. Create a poster alerting young children to the danger of guns suitable for hanging in the hallways of an elementary school.

   c. Design a webpage that would alert elementary-age children to some of the dangers of guns and inform them about some relevant statistics.

3. Writing texts for a resistant audience:

   a. Write a letter to the National Rifle Association asking it to endorse a statewide ban on automatic weapons and handguns.

   b. Find fault with several of the statistics in the Youth and Violence in America Fact Sheet. Write a response to the National Center for Education Statistics identifying aspects of the data that you consider tainted, sensationalistic, or inaccurate. Support why you think the data are negative and give some idea as to the legitimate figures.

   c. You are representing the United States in a junior United Nations. Several countries, most notably representatives from France, Japan, Iraq, and Sudan, cite the prevalence of violence in schools as evidence that U.S. citizens are genetically more violent than those from other countries. You want to combat their views by presenting data in such a way that these individuals will no longer perceive violence in schools as evidence of a predisposition for violence in U.S. citizens.

From *Going Bohemian: How to Teach Writing Like You Mean It* (2nd edition) by Lawrence Baines & Anthony Kunkel. Copyright 2010 International Reading Association.